how2become

QTS NUMERACY TESTS

www.How2Become.com

by Richard McMunn

As part of this product you have also received **FREE** access to online tests that will help you to pass QTS Numeracy tests

To gain access, simply go to:

www.PsychometricTestsOnline.co.uk

Get more products for passing any test or interview at:

www.how2become.com

Orders: Please contact How2become Ltd, Suite 3, 50 Churchill Square Business Centre, Kings Hill, Kent ME19 4YU. You can also order via the e mail address info@how2become.co.uk.

ISBN: 978-1-910602-34-8

First published in 2014 by How2Become Ltd

Typeset for How2become Ltd by Anton Pshinka.

Printed in Great Britain for How2become Ltd by CMP.

CONTENTS OF YOUR GUIDE

INTRODUCTION TO YOUR NEW GUIDE

Dear Sir/Madam,

Welcome to your new guide, QTS Numeracy Tests. This guide contains lots of sample test questions that are appropriate for anyone who is preparing to sit the Numeracy Skills Test which is a requirement before enrolling on to the Initial Teacher Training (ITT) course.

The key to success in any career or job-related assessment is to try your hardest to get 100% in the test that you are undertaking. If you aim for 100% in your preparation, then you are far more likely to achieve the trade or career that you want. We have deliberately supplied you with lots of sample questions to assist you. It is crucial that when you get a question wrong, you take the time to find out why you got it wrong. Understanding the question is very important.

Finally, if you want to try out more tests that will prepare you for your assessment, then we offer a wide range of products to assist you at www.how2become.com. We have also provided you with some additional free online psychometric tests which will help to further improve your competence in this particular testing area. To gain access, simply go to:

www.PsychometricTestsOnline.co.uk

Good luck and best wishes,

The how2become team

The How2become team

PREFACE BY AUTHOR RICHARD MCMUNN

It's probably important that I start off by explaining a little bit about myself, my background, and why I'm suitably qualified to help you prepare for your QTS Numerical test.

At the time of writing I am 42 years old and live in Tunbridge Wells, Kent. I left school at the usual age of 16 and joined the Royal Navy, serving on-board HMS Invincible as part of 800 Naval Air Squadron which formed part of the Fleet Air Arm. There I was, at the age of 16, travelling the world and working as an engineer on Sea Harrier jets! It was fantastic and I loved every minute of it. After four years I left the Royal Navy and joined Kent Fire and Rescue Service as a Firefighter.

Over the next 17 years I worked my way up through the ranks to the position of Assistant Divisional Officer. During my time in the Fire Service I spent a lot of time working as an instructor at the Fire Brigade Training Centre. I was also involved in the selection process for assessing candidates who wanted to join the Fire Service as a Firefighter. Therefore, my knowledge and experience gained so far in life has been invaluable in helping people like you to pass any type of selection process. I am sure you will find this testing guide an invaluable resource during your preparation for your numeracy skills assessment.

I have always been fortunate in the fact that I persevere at everything I do. I understand that if I keep working hard in life then I will always be successful, or I will achieve whatever it is that I want to achieve. This is an important lesson that I want you to take on-board straight away. If you work hard and persevere, then success will come your way. It is also very important that you believe in your own abilities.

Finally, as part of this product I want to give you FREE access to online tests that will help you pass any numerical assessment. To gain access, simply go to:

www.PsychometricTestsOnline.co.uk

Best wishes,

Richard McMunn

Richard McMunn

DISCLAIMER

ABOUT THE QTS NUMERACY TEST

The QTS Numerical test is required for entry to become an initial teacher. As a teacher, you will need to demonstrate a high level of ability in numeracy in all areas of work in school. This set of standards applies to ALL teachers, not just those who teach subjects which include numerical ability, such as mathematics. It is vital that you are fully prepared for the tests and the first stage in your preparation is to gain an understanding of what is involved during the tests.

The tests are a mandatory assessment which MUST be passed, in order to demonstrate a range of practical skills deemed most important for a teacher's general professional practice. The Teaching Agency will hold a number of test forms in each subject area and you will be assigned a test paper, picked at random, when you enter the test. Because the test paper is picked at random, there is no way of determining the type of questions you will be asked; therefore, it is vital you prepare for every eventuality and type of question.

The test papers and questions that are held by the Teaching Agency are changed and renewed each year. All tests are piloted each year by the Teaching Agency to ensure that they are relevant to the role and are of a standard that is comparable to the teaching role in which you are expected to undertake. The tests themselves are taken in a secure test centre, on a computer, unless special arrangements have been granted for an alternative format. In addition to using this manual and the test questions contained within it, we also recommend you take the time to work through the bank of practice tests and support information that is made available to you on the Teaching Agency pages of the Department for Education website.

The numeracy test that you will be required to undertake consists of a variety of different contexts and situations that are relevant to the teaching role. The contexts and situations come from a wide range of sources including documents issued by government agencies and schools. The questions themselves will present positive contexts and pay attention to the issues of equality and diversity in the choice of names and scenarios etc.

Structure and format of the numeracy test

The numeracy skills test is a computerised test covering three separate areas: mental arithmetic, interpreting and using written data, and solving written arithmetic problems. You will only have a total of 48 minutes to complete the test unless you have specifically requested special arrangements to be made.

Audio (mental arithmetic) questions

To begin with, there is a mental arithmetic section which comprises of an audio test which you listen to through provided headphones. This area of the test will assess your mental competence in the following key areas:

- Time;
- Fractions;
- Percentages;
- Measurements;
- Conversions.

During this section each of the questions are individually-timed and you are not allowed to use a calculator.

Written numeracy questions

During this part of the numeracy skills test you will need to answer computer-based questions. You are permitted to use a calculator during this test but not your own. An on-screen calculator will be provided. The test questions will assess your ability to interpret and use written data in the following key areas:

- Identifying trends correctly;
- Making comparisons in order to draw conclusions;
- Interpreting information accurately.

You will also be tested on your ability to solve written arithmetic problems which are set in a variety of situations and will include:

- Time;
- Money;
- Proportion and ratio;
- Percentages, fractions and decimals;
- Measurements (e.g. distance, area);
- Conversions (e.g. from one currency to another, from fractions to decimals or percentages);
- Averages (including mean, median, mode and range where relevant);
- Using simple formulae.

The numeracy skills test format

Each test consists of a total of 28 questions: 12 mental arithmetic and 16 on-screen displayed on the computer screen. All of the questions carry one mark regardless of the number of required responses. All the numeracy tests have been calibrated statistically against a benchmark test. The pass mark for the benchmark test is currently 63 per cent but this can vary. As with any multiple set of tests, the tests are not exactly the same difficulty, but are of an equivalent standard. A test with slightly harder questions will have a slightly lower pass mark and a test with slightly easier questions will have a slightly higher pass mark.

TIPS FOR PASSING THE TESTS

There's no two ways about it, the most effective way in which you can prepare for the tests is to carry out lots of sample test questions. When I say lots, I mean lots! Before I provide you with a host of test questions for you to try, here are a few important tips for you to consider:

- Variety is the key to success. I recommend that you attempt a variety of different testing questions from a range of areas in regards to psycho-metric tests. These should include numerical reasoning, verbal reasoning, fault analysis and mechanical reasoning. This will undoubtedly improve your overall ability to pass the test that you are required to undertake. If you go to the free tests at www.**PsychometricTestsOnline.co.uk** then you will be able to try all of these free of charge.

- During your preparation for the QTS, it is important that you understand why you answered a question incorrectly and how you arrived at your chosen answer. If you take the time to check your answers carefully then this will undoubtedly improve your performance when you sit the real test.

- Confidence is an important part of test preparation. Most people who sit 'timed-tests' find their mind goes blank. Once this happens, they start to panic. This is because their mind is focused on negative thoughts and they end up believing they will fail the test. If you practice plenty of test questions under timed conditions, then your confidence will undoubtedly grow. If your confidence is at its peak at the commencement of the test, then there is no doubt that you will actually look forward to sitting it, as opposed to being fearful of the outcome.

- Whilst this is a very basic tip that appears obvious, many people neglect to follow it. Make sure you get a good nights sleep the night prior to your test or assessment. Research has shown that those people who have regular 'good' sleep are far more likely to concentrate better during psychometric tests.

- During the QTS skills test aim for SPEED as well as ACCURACY. Many test centres want to see how quickly you can work, but they also want to see how accurate your work is too. Therefore, when tackling the tests you must work as quickly as you can without sacrificing accuracy. Most tests nowadays are designed so that you do not finish them; you will also most probably lose marks for incorrect answers and guessing.

- You are what you eat! In the week prior to the test eat and drink healthily. Avoid cigarettes, alcohol and food with high fat content. The reason for this is that all of these will make you feel sluggish and you will not perform at your peak. On the morning of your assessment eat a healthy breakfast such as porridge and a banana.

- Drink plenty of water, always!

- If you have any special needs that need to be catered for, make sure that you inform the assessment centre staff prior to the assessment day. I have met people in the past who are fearful of telling the assessment staff that they are dyslexic. You will not be treated negatively; in fact the exact opposite. They will give you extra time in the tests which can only work in your favour.

Now that I have provided you with a number of important tips, take the time to work through the 30 sample test exercises that follow.

In order to help you further during your preparation we have provided you with a number of further resources and worksheets which explain how to tackle the types of questions you will encounter during the QTS numeracy test. You can download the support package at the following page free of charge:

www.QTSnumeracytests.co.uk

QTS EXAMPLES

We have provided you with detailed examples of all the questions that you will encounter within this guide. Please note, *each example question is the first question taken from each section of the guide.* (There are 30 test sections in the guide, and therefore we have provided you with 30 different examples).

Question 1

There are 21 pupils in a class. 3 of the pupils leave the class to get extra help. What is the fraction of pupils that remain in class? Give your answer in its lowest terms.

How to work it out

Step 1 = 3 people leave the class. The total of the class was 21, and so there will now be 18 pupils left in the class.

Step 2 = As a fraction of pupils that remain in the class, it would be written as 18/21.

Step 3 = (The number of students remaining in the class over the total number of pupils that was originally in the class).

Step 4 = 18/21 in its simplest form = 6/7 (both numbers are divided by 3).

Answer
6/7

Question 2

2500 millilitres of liquid is divided into 20 containers. How many millilitres of liquid does each container have?

How to work it out

Step 1 = 2500 millilitres divided by 20 containers.

Step 2 = 2500 ÷20 = 125.

Answer
125

Question 3

A school trip in Belgium involves walking 24 Km every day.
If 8km is approximately equal to 5 miles, estimate
how many miles the daily walk consists of?

How to work it out

<u>Step 1</u> = 8km = 5 miles.

<u>Step 2</u> = They walk 24 km a day.

<u>Step 3</u> = 24 divided by 8 = 3.

<u>Step 4</u> =So 3 x 5 = 15 miles.

Answer
15 miles

Question 4

A team event consists of 16 tasks. Each task lasts 10 minutes.
How many hours will this team event last in hours and minutes?

How to work it out

<u>Step 1</u> = 16 tasks multiplied by 10 minutes = 160 minutes.

<u>Step 2</u> = 160 minutes in hours and minutes = 2 hours and 40 minutes.

Answer
2 hours and 40 minutes.

Question 5

A Maths lesson begins at 11:50. The teacher introduces the topic for 6 minutes, there is a warm up exercise for 18 minutes and finally work is done on the new topic for the last 26 minutes. When does the lesson end? Give your answer using the 24-hour clock?

How to work it out

<u>Step 1</u> = Add up how many minutes each task takes.

<u>Step 2</u> = 6 + 18 + 26 = 50 minutes.

<u>Step 3</u> = So, if the lesson starts at 11.50, and they are in the lesson for 50 minutes.

<u>Step 4</u> = Their lesson will finish at 12.40.

Answer
12.40

Question 6

A school calculated that it had given merits to boys and girls in the ratio of 4:1.There were a total of 680 merits given. How many merits did the girls get?

How to work it out

<u>Step 1</u> = There were 680 merits in total.

<u>Step 2</u> = The ratio of boys to girls was 4:1.

<u>Step 3</u> = 680 divided by 5 = 136 merits for the girls.

Answer
136

Question 7

In a Junior School there are 240 pupils and 35% have free school dinners. Work out the number of children who do not have free school dinners.

How to work it out

Step 1 = 35% have free school dinners. That means you want to work out the 65% that do not have free school dinners.

Step 2 = So 65% of 240 = 240 ÷ 100 x 65 = 156.

Answer
156

Question 8

220 pupils sat a GCSE Maths exam. The fraction of pupils who get Grade C or above is 3/5. How many pupils get Grade D or below?

How to work it out

Step 1 = 3/5 of pupils get a C grade or above. That means 2/5 of students received a D grade or below.

Step 2 = 220 pupils altogether. Divide it by the bottom number of the fraction (5).

Step 3 = 220 divided by 5 = 44 (that gives you 1/5).

Step 4 = 44 x 2 = 88 people received grade D or below.

Answer
88

Question 9

A pupil scores 45.5% in Test 1 and 64.5% in Test 2. What was the pupil's average mark, assuming they were weighted equally?

How to work it out

Step 1 = To work out the average (or the mean) you add up the totals (45.5 + 64.5) and then divide it by how many totals there are (2).

Step 2 = 45.5 + 64.5 = 110 ÷ 2 = 55%.

Answer
55%

Question 10

There are 11 girls and 14 boys in a class.
What is the percentage of girls in this class?

How to work it out

Step 1 = To work out the percentage of girls you add up the total of girls and boys (25).

Step 2 = 100 (%) divide it by 25 x 11 (multiply by 11 because that is the number of girls you are trying to work out).

Step 3 = 100 ÷ 25 x 11 = 44%.

Answer
44%

Question 11

A primary school has 80 pupils in year 3. 10 pupils have a reading age that is below their actual age. What is the percentage of pupils who have a reading age that is below their actual age? Give your answer to two decimal places.

How to work it out

<u>Step 1</u> = 10 divided by 80 x 100 = 12.5%.

<u>Step 2</u> = 12.5% converted into a decimal (you move the decimal point two spaces to the left).

<u>Step 3</u> = 0.125.

Answer
0.125

Question 12

Two Geography classes get together to watch a video. The first class has 10 boys and 16 girls. The second class has 15 girls and 9 boys. When the class is combined what is the percentage of girls as a proportion of the total number of pupils?

How to work it out

<u>Step 1</u> = Add up all boys and girls. 10 + 16 + 15 + 9 = 50.

<u>Step 2</u> = Out of the 50 pupils, there are 16 + 15 girls = 31.

<u>Step 3</u> = So 31 divided by 50 x 100 – 62% of the class are girls.

Answer
62%

Question 13

In a Science class 2/5 of the pupils achieved a level 5 in Key Stage 2. In another class ½ of the pupils achieve this level. What is the total fraction for both classes combined that achieves this level?

How to work it out

Step 1 = To add fractions, you have to find a number that both numbers can go into.

Step 2 = 5 and 2 both can go into 10 (you want to find the smallest number that they both can go in).

Step 3 = In order to get 10 from 5, we multiplied it by 2, so you have to do the same to the top part of the fraction. 2 x 2 = 4. So the first fraction you have 4/10.

Step 4 = In order to get 10 from 2, we multiplied it by 5, so you have to do the same to the top part of the fraction. 5 x 1 = 5. So the second fraction gives you 5/10. So, 4/10 + 5/10 = 9/10.

Answer
9/10

Question 14

A pupil scored 28%, 47% and 42% respectively in three different maths tests. What was the pupil's mean mark?

How to work it out

Step 1 = To work out the average (or the mean) you add up the totals (28 + 47 + 42) and then divide it by how many totals there are (3).

Step 2 = 28 + 47 + 42 = 117.

Step 3 = 117 ÷ 3 = 39%.

Answer
39%

Question 15

What is 12.5% of 380 kilograms?

How to work it out

<u>Step 1</u> = 12.5% of 380.

<u>Step 2</u> = 380 ÷ 100 x 12.5 = 47.5.

Answer
47.5

Question 16

A school day ends at 3.30pm. In the afternoon there are only
2 sessions of 45 minutes with a 5 minute break in between.
When does the afternoon session start?

How to work it out

<u>Step 1</u> = Two sessions in the afternoon of 45 minutes each. 45 x 2 = 90.

<u>Step 2</u> = 90 + 5 minute break = 95 minutes.

<u>Step 3</u> = 95 minutes = 1 hour and 35 minutes.

<u>Step 4</u> = 3.30pm – 1 hour and 35 minutes = 13.55pm.

Answer
13.55pm

Question 17

A History class joins a Science class for a school trip. The total number of pupils in this trip is 49. If 3/7 of the pupils were from the Science class, how many pupils were there from the History class?

How to work it out

Step 1 = If 3/7 of the pupils were from the science class, which means 4/7 are from the history class.

Step 2 = So, 49 pupils in total divided by 7 = 7 x 4 = 28 pupils are from the history class.

Answer
28

Question 18

A coach can accommodate 54 people. There are 36 pupils who go on a school outing in this coach. During the outing there has to be one teacher for every 6 pupils. How many vacant seats are there?

How to work it out

Step 1 = There are 36 pupils attending the trip.

Step 2 = For every 6 pupils there has to be one teacher.

Step 3 = 36 divided by 6 = 6 teachers.

Step 4 = 36 pupils + 6 teachers + 42 people.

Step 5 = There is 54 seats. So, the number of vacant seats is 54 – 42 = 12.

Answer
12

Question 19

A teacher needs to write reports in her subject for 32 pupils. Each report will take her an average of 9 minutes to write. She also spends an average of 4 minutes checking each report. How long in hours and minutes does it take the teacher to finish the entire report writing tasks?

How to work it out

Step 1 = In total it takes 13 minutes to look at one report.

Step 2 = The teacher has 32 reports to write.

Step 3 = 32 reports x 13 minutes (each) = 416 minutes.

Step 4 = 416 minutes = 6 hours and 56 minutes.

Answer
6 hours and 56 minutes

Question 20

What is 454 divided by 0.2?

How to work it out

Step 1 = If you were dividing by 0.1, you would simply add a 0.

Step 2 = To get 0.2, you would half the answer you got for 0.1

Step 3 = 4540 divided by 2 = 2270.

Answer
2270

Question 21

The lowest score on a Maths test is 53. The highest score is 92.
The median score is 71. The lower quartile is 56 and the upper quartile is 87.
Represent this information with a box-and-whisker plot.

How to work it out

Step 1 = The lowest score forms the first line. The highest score forms the last line. The median score is the line in the middle of the box. The lower interquartile is the lower section of the box and the upper quartile forms the upper part of the box.

Answer
Your answer should look something like this:

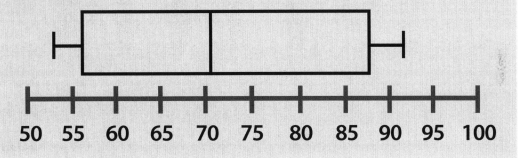

Question 22

Test marks in Maths, History and English for Year 9 are compared by three box – and – whisker diagrams shown below.
Marks are shown on the vertical axis.

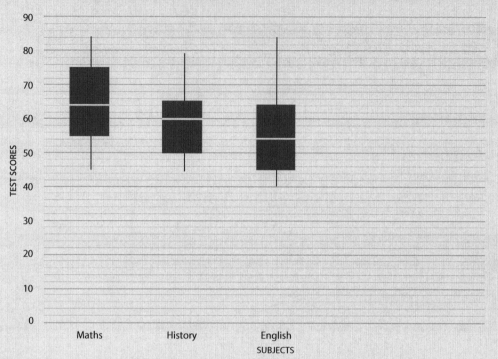

How to work it out

Question 1 = The interquartile range for Maths is higher than that for English. True or false?

Question 2 = The lowest mark was in History. True or false?

Question 3 = The median score for Maths is 65. True or false?

Answers
1. True (work out the difference between the lower and higher quartiles).
2. False = (lowest mark was in English).
3. False (The median score was 64).

Question 23

The set of data below shows the results in a year 9 History test for 50 pupils. The marks are out of 10. The teacher wants to find the mean mark for this test. Give your answer to 1 decimal place.

Marks in History Test	No. of pupils	No. of pupils X History Marks
1	5	1 X 5 = 5
2	1	2 X 1 = 2
3	8	
4	2	
5	7	
6	6	
7	3	
8	11	
9	4	
10	3	
Totals	50	

How to work it out

Step 1 = In order to work this out, you have to fill in the last column, like shown in the previous two boxes.

Step 2 = You then add up the answers in the last column.

Step 3 = Divide that number by the number of pupils (Total of History marks divided by number of pupils).

Step 4 = 5.7 is the average mark.

Answer
5.7

Question 24

A Mock exam in Science consists of two papers. The first paper is out of 50 and has weighting of 75% given to it. The second paper is out of 40 and has a weighting of 25% given to it. A pupil gets 44 in the first paper and 27 in the second paper. What is the pupil's final percentage score? Give your answer to 1 decimal place.

How to work it out

<u>Step 1</u> = First paper = 44 (marks) divide it by 50 (total of marks) multiply it by 75% (percentage weight) – 66.

<u>Step 2</u> = Second paper = 27 ÷ 40 x 25 = 16.875.

<u>Step 3</u> = 66 + 16.875 = 82.875.

<u>Step 4</u> = To one decimal place = 82.9%.

Answer
82.9%

Question 25

The two way table shown compares pupils' results for GCSE Maths with GCSE Science grades.

| Maths GCSE Grades | Science GCSE Grades | | | | | | | | |
	A*	A	B	C	D	E	F	U	Total
A*									
A			3						3
B	1	2	4	2	3				12
C		2	3	10	2	2		1	20
D			2	3					5
E									
F									
U									
Total		1	4	12	15	5	2		1	40

How to work it out

Question 1 = The number of pupils who achieved a C grade in both Science and Maths is 3. True or false?

Question 2 = The number of pupils who got a B grade in Maths is 12. True or false?

Question 3 = The percentage of pupils who received a C grade in Science is approximately 37.5%. True or false?

Answers
1. False (number of pupils would be 10)
2. True
3. True

Question 26

The pie chart below shows the number of pupils who got a Grade C or better in Science in three different schools.

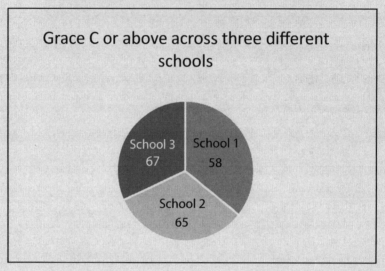

Grace C or above across three different schools

How to work it out

<u>Question 1</u> = The percentage of pupils who got a grade C or above in Science in School 1 compared to all the schools combined was approximately 30.5%. True or false?

<u>Question 2</u> = The total percentage success at Grade C or above in Science at School 1 and School 2 combined compared to all schools was approximately 64.7%. True or false?

<u>Question 3</u> = The proportion of pupils getting a grade C or above in Science at School 3 compared to all schools was 67/190. True or false?

Answers
1. True (58 ÷ 190 x 100)
2. True (58+65 ÷ 190 x 100)
3. True

Question 27

*Pupils who succeeded in getting Maths GCSE at Grade C
or above were analysed from 2006 to 2012.*

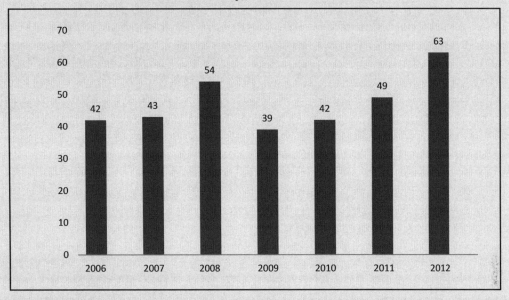

How to work it out

Question 1 = The percentage of GCSE at grades C or above increased every year. True or false?

Question 2 = The mean percentage from 2009 to 2012 was 48.25%. True or false?

Question 3 = The difference from the lowest percentage of pupils received a Maths GCSE at C grade or above to the highest is 24. True or false?

Answers
1. False (it decreases in year 2009)
2. True (39+42+49+63) ÷ 4)
3. True (lowest was 39, highest was 63, so the difference is 24)

Question 28

The head of English created the following table showing the number of pupils in each year group who had additional help in English. What is the percentage of pupils in all the year groups combined that are having additional tuition. Give your answer rounded to a whole number.

Year Group	No. of pupils	No. of pupils receiving additional help in English
7	96	15
8	108	21
9	111	16
10	98	9
11	116	15

How to work it out

<u>Step 1</u> = Add up total number of pupils.

<u>Step 2</u> = Add up no. of pupils receiving addition English help.

<u>Step 3</u> = 76 ÷ 529 = 14% (as a whole number).

Answer
14%

Question 29

Maths GCSE grades were recorded for 40 pupils. The data is shown on a cumulative frequency diagram below. Indicate all true statements below:

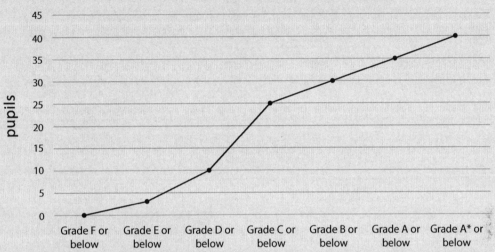

Maths GCSE grades recorded for 40 pupils

How to work it out

Question 1 = 15 pupils get above Grade C. True or false?

Question 2 = 30 pupils get above Grade D. True or false?

Question 3 = 50% of the 40 pupils get a C Grade or above. True or false?

Answers
1. True (the dot on the line C grade or below is on 25.
There are 40 pupils. 40 – 25 = 15)
2. True (the dot on the line D grade or below is on 10.
There are 40 pupils. 40 – 10= 30)
3. False (only 15 people get a C grade or above.
There are 40 pupils, therefore is not 50%)

Question 30

A teacher represents the relationship between marks in a maths test and an English test by the scatter graph shown below. The Maths marks are out of 50 and the English marks are out of 20. Indicate all true statements below:

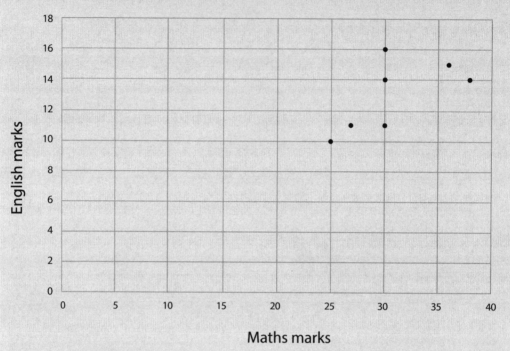

Maths marks

How to work it out

<u>Question 1</u> = The correlation between Maths and English marks in this test was negative. True or false?

<u>Question 2</u> = When the pupils mark in Maths was 25, there mark in English was 10. True or false?

<u>Question 3</u> = The mean mark in the Maths test was approximately 31. True or false?

Answers
1. False (it's positive not negative, as the English marks increase, the maths marks increase)
2. True
3. True (25+27+30+30+30+36+38 = 216 ÷ 7 = 30.8, rounded up 31)

QTS NUMERACY TEST
SECTION 1

There are 25 questions in this sample test section and you have 12 minutes to complete them. You should be aiming to achieve a minimum of 16 correct answers from the 25 questions that are available.

QTS NUMERACY TEST SECTION 1

Question 1

There are 21 pupils in a class. 3 of the pupils leave the class to get extra help. What is the fraction of pupils that remain in class? Give your answer in its lowest terms.

Answer

Question 2

There are 25 pupils in a class. 5 pupils have been moved from the bottom group of Literacy to the top group of Literacy. What percentage of pupils have been moved up?

Answer

Question 3

100 students took part in an online assessment. 10% of students failed to achieve a C grade. How many students failed to achieve a C grade?

Answer

Question 4

65 pupils took part in sports day. There are 143 pupils who attend the school. What is the fraction of pupils that took part in sports day over the number of pupils who attend the school? Give your answer in its lowest terms.

Answer

Question 5

There are 240 pupils at a secondary school. Three quarters of students achieved A-C grades in the year 2013. How many students did not achieve an A-C grade in 2013?

Answer

Question 6

A school has 3 classes going on a school trip on the same day. The school has 416 students. Each class has 32 students. What is the fraction of students who will not be attending a school trip? Give your answer in its lowest terms.

Answer

Question 7

There are 42 students in a class. 6 students receive an award for their outstanding work in Mathematics. What is the fraction of students who received an award in that class? Give your answer in its lowest terms.

Answer

Question 8

A school arranges a bike marathon. 120 pupils take part. 1/3 of pupils finish the race in less than half an hour. How many pupils did not finish the race in less than half an hour?

Answer

Question 9

A school arranges a trip to Thorpe Park. There are 80 pupils attending the trip. 1 adult is needed for every 5 students. How many adults will be needed for the trip to accommodate all the pupils?

Answer [   ]

Question 10

A class has 32 pupils. 8 pupils are struggling to meet the criteria in terms of their grades. What fraction of the class is not struggling with their grades? Give your answer in its lowest terms.

Answer [   ]

Question 11

260 pupils sit a GCSE English exam. ¾ of the pupils who sit the exam get a C grade or above. How many pupils get a D grade or below?

Answer [   ]

Question 12

There are 24 pupils taking part in a GCSE dance exam. 6 pupils achieve an A grade in their dance examination. What is the fraction of pupils who did not achieve an A grade in their GCSE dance exam? Give your answer in its lowest terms.

Answer [   ]

Question 13

63 students are taking part in a school charity event. The charity event is a

school bake sale. 2/3 of the students baked their cakes as opposed to buying them. How many students bought their cakes?

Answer

Question 14

21 students took part in a Science experiment. Only 3 students got the experiment correct first time. What is the fraction of students who got the experiment correct the first time?

Answer

Question 15

There are 36 pupils in a P.E lesson. They are playing tennis. However, 4 students are made to run laps because of mischievous behaviour. What is the fraction of pupils that remain in the lesson playing tennis? Give your answer in its lowest terms.

Answer

Question 16

There are 42 pupils in a class. 6 pupils stay behind after school to catch up with some work. What is the fraction of the pupils that remain after school from that class? Give your answer in its lowest terms.

Answer

Question 17

There are 15 pupils in homework club. 3 pupils manage to complete all their homework in that one hour period. What fraction of pupils are yet to complete all their homework in homework club? Give your answer in its lowest terms.

Answer

Question 18

There are 68 pupils in Year 6. 44 pupils receive free hot school dinners. What fraction of pupils in Year 6 do not receive free hot school dinners? Give your answer in its lowest terms.

Answer

Question 19

45 students take part in the egg and spoon race. 3/5 of students drop their egg at least once. How many students did not drop their egg?

Answer

Question 20

There are 54 pupils taking part in a school talent contest. Only 2/3 of the pupils can make it to the next stage of the competition. How many pupils do not make it through to the next stage of the talent competition?

Answer

Question 21

There are 28 pupils in a Science lesson. Only 2/7 of the pupils are allowed to take part in one experiment at a time. How many pupils take part in one experiment?

Answer

Question 22

There are 136 students attending a school. 1/8 of the pupils are in the school choir. How many students are in the school choir?

Answer [   ]

Question 23

A Media class has 36 pupils. 6 pupils are allowed to leave the classroom and use the media equipment to film for their practical project. What fraction of pupils are left in the classroom? Give your answer in its lowest terms.

Answer [   ]

Question 24

An English class has 24 students. 1/3 of students are off sick on the same day. How many students are left in the class?

Answer [   ]

Question 25

A secondary school has a total of 168 students studying for their GCSEs. 3/7 of students chose Media as one of their GCSE's. How many students decide to study Media for their GCSE?

Answer [   ]

Now check your answers before moving on to the next section of the guide.

ANSWERS TO QTS NUMERACY TEST SECTION 1

1. 6/7

2. 20%

3. 10

4. 5/11

5. 60

6. 10/13

7. 1/7

8. 80

9. 16

10. 3/4

11. 65

12. 3/4

13. 21

14. 1/7

15. 8/9

16. 1/7

17. 4/5

18. 6/17

19. 18

20. 18

21. 8

22. 17

23. 5/6

24. 16

25. 72

QTS NUMERACY TEST
SECTION 2

There are 25 questions in this sample test section and you have 12 minutes to complete them. You should be aiming to achieve a minimum of 16 correct answers from the 25 questions that are available.

QTS NUMERACY TEST SECTION 2

Question 1

2500 millilitres of liquid is divided into 20 containers. How many millilitres of liquid does each container have?

Answer [   ]

Question 2

18 pints of liquid is divided into 3 containers. How many pints of liquid does each container contain?

Answer [   ]

Question 3

A bowl contains 2600 millilitres of fruit juice. The fruit juice needs to fill 130 containers. How many millilitres of fruit juice does each container contain, if you were to divide the juice equally?

Answer [   ]

Question 4

There is 4000 millilitres of water in jugs. How many litres of water are there?

Answer [   ]

Question 5

A school disco is expecting 100 students to attend. Per cup, it holds 250 millilitres. How many litres will be needed to fill the cups if all 100 students were to have 2 cups each?

Answer [   ]

Question 6

One container contains 2 pints. If there are 86 containers, how many pints will there be altogether?

Answer [   ]

Question 7

A school supplies 60,000 millilitres of water. How many litres does the school supply?

Answer [   ]

Question 8

50000 millilitres is divided into 125 containers. How many millilitres does each container contain?

Answer [   ]

Question 9

A pint of milk is equal to two cups. If there were 16 pints of milk, how many cups would that fill?

Answer [   ]

Question 10

A student has to take their medication prescribed by their doctor. She is pre-scribed a 10.5 fluid ounce bottle of medication with the instructions to take 0.25 fluid ounces twice a day. How many days/weeks does she have to take the medication for?

Answer [   ]

Question 11

A school holds a disco for 50 pupils. A quart of orange juice is the same as 4 cups. If each pupil had 4 cups of orange juice, how many quarts would be needed?

Answer [ ]

Question 12

A cup of water can hold 8 fluid ounces. If a school supplied 120 pupils with one cup of water at break time, how many fluid ounces would be needed?

Answer [ ]

Question 13

A gallon is the same as 16 cups, equivalent to 8 pints, or 4 quarts. If there was 18 gallons of water, work out what that would be in cups, pints and quarts.

Answer [ ]

Question 14

A school is expecting 100 students to attend a charity event. They are offering drinks. Per cup, it holds 250 millilitres. How many cups would be needed if the school had 40,000 millilitres of water?

Answer [ ]

Question 15

A jug has exactly 1 litre of water in it. In the dining hall of a school there are 25 tables with two jugs on each table. How many litres of water are there in total?

Answer [ ]

Question 16

A container contains 2 pints. If there was 120 pints, how many containers would be needed in order to contain all 120 pints?

Answer

Question 17

A pint of milk is equivalent to 2 cups. If there was 346 cups to fill, how many pints of milk would be needed?

Answer

Question 18

If 1 litre is equivalent to 1000 millilitres, how many litres would you have if there was 50000 millilitres?

Answer

Question 19

A gallon is the equivalent to 16 cups, 8 pints or 4 quarts. Work out how many cups, pints and quarts it would make if you had 50 gallons.

Answer

Question 20

Each cup can contain 300 millilitres of water. A school decides to put on a charity event for parents. They are expecting 220 parents to attend. If the students were to offer two cups of water per parent, how many millilitres of water would they need?

Answer

Question 21

120 pints is divided into 30 containers. How many pints does each container contain?

Answer [   ]

Question 22

There are 3,600 millilitres of water which needs to be divided into 20 containers. How many millilitres does each container contain?

Answer [   ]

Question 23

A teacher has been prescribed medication by her doctor. She is prescribed a 10.5 fluid ounce bottle of medication with the instructions to take 0.25 fluid ounces three times a day. How many days/weeks does she have to take the medication for?

Answer [   ]

Question 24

A school holds a charity event for 120 students. If a quart of juice is equivalent to 4 cups, how many cups would be needed if there was 200 quarts of orange juice?

Answer [   ]

Question 25

There is 16000 millilitres of water in jugs. How many litres of water are there?

Answer [   ]

Now check your answers before moving on to the next section of the guide.

ANSWERS TO QTS NUMERACY TEST SECTION 2

1. 125

2. 6

3. 20

4. 4

5. 50

6. 172

7. 60

8. 400

9. 32

10. 3 weeks/ 21 days

11. 50

12. 960 fluid ounces

13. 288 cups/ 144 pints/ 72 quarts

14. 160

15. 50

16. 60

17. 173

18. 50

19. 800 cups / 400 pints / 200 quarts

20. 132,000 millilitres

21. 4

22. 180

23. 2 weeks/ 14 days

24. 800

25. 16

QTS NUMERACY TEST
SECTION 3

There are 25 questions in this sample test section and you have 12 minutes to complete them. You should be aiming to achieve a minimum of 16 correct answers from the 25 questions that are available.

QTS NUMERACY TEST SECTION 3

Question 1

A school trip to Belgium involves walking 24 km per day. If 8 km is approximately equal to 5 miles, estimate how many miles the daily walk consists of?

Answer (miles) [   ]

Question 2

A school arranges a bike ride for students in order to raise money for charity. The bike ride is 32 kilometres long. If 1km is approximately 0.6 miles, how many whole miles will the bike ride consist of?

Answer [   ]

Question 3

A school puts on a fun walk for students in the summer. A kilometre is equal to 1,000 metres. The walk is approximately 4,000 metres long. How many kilometres are the students going to walk?

Answer [   ]

Question 4

Teachers get their students to measure the school playground using centimetres and metres. The playground was measured to be 34 metres long. How many centimetres does the playground measure out to be?

Answer [   ]

Question 5

A school plans a trip to Northern Ireland. The trip involves walking 16km a day for 4 days. If 8km is approximately equivalent to 5 miles, how many miles are the students walking in total?

Answer [   ]

Question 6

Students are told that 1 kilometre is equivalent to 1000 metres. How many metres would 130 kilometres be?

Answer [   ]

Question 7

Students measure the distance from point A to point B for a class experiment. They measure the distance using metres. If 100 centimetres is 1 metre, and the students measured the distance as being 3000 centimetres, how many metres did they measure?

Answer [   ]

Question 8

A school arranges a trip to Thorpe Park. One of the rides is 205 feet high. There are approximately 13 inches in 1 foot. How high, in inches, is the ride?

Answer [   ]

Question 9

A school takes part in a series of bicycle half marathons. It is approximately 13 miles per half marathon. How many miles in total would they be riding if they took part in 3 half marathons?

Answer

Question 10

A school organises a fun run. A kilometre is equivalent to 1000 metres. If the students were to run 6000 metres, how many kilometres would they be running?

Answer

Question 11

18 students take part in an endurance challenge over 3 days. 8 kilometres is approximately 5 miles. The students take part in 3 challenges. A 24km walk, a 16km bike ride and an 8km swim. How many miles across the 3 challenges are the students enduring?

Answer

Question 12

Students are attending a class where they are learning about measurements. They learn that 100 centimetres is 1 metre. How many centimetres would there be in 150 metres?

Answer

Question 13

A school decides to go on a school trip to Germany. They are going to walk 35 miles in 7 days. If 1 mile is equal to 0.6 kilometres, how many kilometres in total will the students walk?

Answer [   ]

Question 14

How many metres are there in 50 ¼ km?

Answer [   ]

Question 15

Which of the following is the least distance? 100,000 x 30cm wooden rulers or the height of Mount Everest, which is 8,848m above sea level?

Answer [   ]

Question 16

22 teachers from a school take part in a charity event. They take part in 3 activities. A 4km walk around the countryside, an 8km bike ride and a 16km run to finish. If 8km is approximately 5 miles, how many miles will the teachers be enduring over the 3 activities?

Answer [   ]

Question 17

How many metres are there in 20 ¾ km?

Answer [   ]

Question 18

A school puts on a cross country run. A kilometre is equivalent to 1000 metres. If the students were to run 9000 metres, how many kilometres would they be running?

Answer [   ]

Question 19

A centimetre is equivalent to 10 millimetres. How many centimetres is 15000 millilitres?

Answer [   ]

Question 20

How many metres are there in 40 ½ km?

Answer [   ]

Question 21

Which is the greater distance? A 3km walk or a 5000m bike ride?

Answer [   ]

Question 22

A school arranges a relay for students in order to raise money for a charity. The relay in total is 48 kilometres long, with 4 students in a team. If 8km is approximately 5 miles, how many miles will each student be running?

Answer [   ]

Question 23

A school trip to Italy is taking place. The trip will involve a 4km boat ride daily. They are going on the same boat for 3 days. If 8km is approximately equivalent to 5 miles, how many miles will the students be travelling across the 3 days?

Answer [   ]

Question 24

Students measure the distance from point A to point B for a class experiment. They measure the distance using metres. If 100 centimetres is 1 metre, and the students measured the distance as being 8000 centimetres, how many metres did they measure?

Answer [   ]

Question 25

A school arranges a walk for students in order to raise money for a charity event. The bike ride is 15 miles long. If 8km is approximately 5 miles, how many kilometres will the walk consist of?

Answer [   ]

Now check your answers before moving onto the next section of the guide.

ANSWERS TO QTS NUMERACY TEST SECTION 3

1. 15 miles

2. 19 miles

3. 4

4. 3400

5. 40 miles

6. 130000

7. 30

8. 2665

9. 39

10. 6

11. 30 miles

12. 15000

13. 21

14. 50,250 metres

15. The height of Mount Everest above sea level which is 8,848m

16. 17.5 miles

17. 20,750 metres

18. 9

19. 1500

20. 40500 metres

21. 5000m bike ride

22. 7.5 miles each

23. 7.5 miles

24. 80 metres

25. 24 kilometres

QTS NUMERACY TEST
SECTION 4

There are 25 questions in this sample test section and you have 12 minutes to complete them. You should be aiming to achieve a minimum of 16 correct answers from the 25 questions that are available.

QTS NUMERACY TEST SECTION 4

Question 1

A team event consists of 16 tasks. Each task lasts 10 minutes. How long will this team event last for in hours and minutes?

Answer

Question 2

A school event consists of 12 tasks. Each task takes approximately 15 minutes. How long will the team event last? Give your answer in hours.

Answer

Question 3

A charity event is taking place at a local school. The event consists of 6 events per day across a 3 day period. Each event takes 30 minutes long. In total, how many hours will the whole charity event take?

Answer

Question 4

In a school day, there are 5 lessons. Each lesson is 50 minutes long. How long are students in lessons for per day? Give your answer in hours and minutes.

Answer

Question 5

A P.E lesson lasts for 50 minutes. They have 3 P.E lessons a week. How many hours are students in P.E lessons across 3 weeks?

Answer

Question 6

In an hour's Science lesson, the teacher introduces 3 tasks in which the students must complete before the end of the lesson. The first task should take 10 minutes, the second task should take 25 minutes and the third task should take 15 minutes. How many minutes are left before the end of the lesson?

Answer [   ]

Question 7

Students are sitting their GCSE English examination. It's a 2 hour long exam. There are 2 sections to the exam. Planning takes approximately 10 minutes per section. There are 2 questions to answer in each section. If the student was to divide their time evenly for each question, how many minutes per question will they have to write their answers (minus the planning time)?

Answer [   ]

Question 8

A student is given 3 tasks for the day. Each task is 25 minutes long. In total, how long will it take for the student to complete the 3 tasks? Give your answer in hours and minutes

Answer [   ]

Question 9

A school detention lasts an hour. A student has 3 sets of homework to complete. How long approximately does he have for each set of homework, if he were to complete all his homework in one detention?

Answer [   ]

Question 10

A local school is having their sports day. Sports day consists of 12 sporting events. Each event takes approximately 20 minutes. In total, how long will sports day last? Give your answer in hours and minutes.

Answer [   ]

Question 11

A local school has introduced the Chinese language to their academic studies. They are going to teach the lesson twice a week. Each lesson is 45 minutes long. How many hours will students be learning Chinese over the 6 week period?

Answer [   ]

Question 12

In a school day, students get 2 breaks and a lunch break. Each break is 15 minutes and lunch is 45 minutes. How long do students get in total for break and lunch times? Give your answer in minutes.

Answer [   ]

Question 13

In a Media lesson, the lesson is split into 3 sections. The first section will be a 15 minute introduction, the second section will be planning for 20 minutes and the last stage will be for filming. The lesson is an hour long. How long do students get for the filming stage?

Answer [   ]

Question 14

An Art examination is 3 hours long. They have 4 sections to complete. If they divided their time equally, how long will the student spend on each section of the examination?

Answer [   ]

Question 15

A school detention is 75 minutes long. A student has 5 sets of homework to complete. How long approximately does he have for each set of homework, if he were to complete all his homework in one detention?

Answer [   ]

Question 16

Students are sitting their GCSE History examination. The exam lasts for 150 minutes. There are 2 sections to the exam. Planning takes approximately 15 minutes per section. There are 3 questions to answer in each section. If the student was to divide their time evenly for each question, how many minutes per question will they have? (deduct planning time).

Answer [   ]

Question 17

A student is given 6 tasks for the day. Each task is 20 minutes long. In total, how long will it take for the student to complete the 6 tasks? Give your answer in minutes.

Answer [   ]

Question 18

In an hour's Geography lesson, the teacher introduces 4 tasks in which the students must complete before the end of the lesson. The first task should take 10 minutes, the second task should take 25 minutes, and the third task should take 10 minutes. How many minutes do the students have to complete the last task?

Answer [   ]

Question 19

A school event consists of 8 tasks. Each task takes approximately 15 minutes. How long will the school event last? Give your answer in hours.

Answer [   ]

Question 20

An event is taking place at a local school. The event consists of 5 events per day across a 4 day period. Each event takes 25 minutes long. In total, how long will the whole charity event take? Give your answer in hours and minutes.

Answer [   ]

Question 21

A local school has introduced the Japanese language to their academic criteria. They are going to teach the lesson 3 times a week. Each lesson is 45 minutes long. How long will students be learning Japanese over 5 weeks? Give your answer in hours and minutes.

Answer [   ]

Question 22

In a Film studies lesson, the lesson is split into 3 sections. The first section will be a 10 minute planning section, the second section will be answering questions for 15 minutes and the last stage will be for filming. The lesson is 50 minutes long. How long do students get for the filming stage?

Answer

Question 23

A student is given 7 tasks for the day. Each task is 15 minutes long. In total, how long will it take for the student to complete the 7 tasks? Give your answer in hours and minutes.

Answer

Question 24

In a school day, there are 6 lessons. Each lesson is 50 minutes long. How long are students in lessons for? Give your answer in hours.

Answer

Question 25

A Technology examination is 3 hours long. They have 3 sections to complete. If they divided their time equally, how long will the student spend on each section of the examination?

Answer

Now check your answers before moving onto the next section of the guide.

ANSWERS TO QTS NUMERACY TEST SECTION 4

1. 2 hours and 40 minutes

2. 3 hours

3. 9 hours

4. 4 hours and 10 minutes

5. 7 hours and 30 minutes

6. 10 minutes

7. 25 minutes

8. 1 hour and 15 minutes

9. 20 minutes

10. 4 hours

11. 9 hours

12. 75 minutes

13. 25 minutes

14. 45 minutes per section

15. 15 minutes

16. 20 minutes

17. 120 minutes

18. 15 minutes

19. 2 hours

20. 8 hours and 20 minutes

21. 11 hours and 15 minutes

22. 25 minutes

23. 1 hour and 45 minutes

24. 5 hours

25. 1 hour per section

QTS NUMERACY TEST
SECTION 5

There are 25 questions in this sample test section and you have 12 minutes to complete them. You should be aiming to achieve a minimum of 16 correct answers from the 25 questions that are available.

QTS NUMERACY TEST SECTION 5

Question 1

A Maths lesson begins at 11:50. The teacher introduces the topic for 6 minutes, there is a warm up exercise for 18 minutes and the last 26 minutes is spent on their assignments. When does the lesson end? Give your answer using the 24-hour clock?

Answer [   ]

Question 2

A Science lesson begins at 09:50. The teacher introduces the topic for 12 minutes, there is a warm up exercise for 25 minutes and the final task is completed in the last 30 minutes. When does the lesson end? Give your answer using the 24-hour clock.

Answer [   ]

Question 3

Lessons begin at 08.50. They have 3 lessons at 75 minutes long and a 15 minute break before lunch starts. What time does lunch time begin?

Answer [   ]

Question 4

A P.E lesson is 90 minutes long. They warm up for 10 minutes and have a cool down for 15 minutes. How many minutes do they spend playing the actual game?

Answer [   ]

Question 5

An English lesson starts at 10.30am. They spend 15 minutes on poetry, 25 minutes on a novel and 10 minutes recapping what they have learned. What time does the class finish?

Answer [   ]

Question 6

A History lesson begins at 10.50am. The teacher introduces the topic for 12 minutes. They have 3 tasks to complete by the end of the lesson. The lesson is an hour long. How long approximatley do the students have for each task if they were to split their time evenly?

Answer [   ]

Question 7

A Dance lesson begins at 10.50am. The teacher introduces the topic for 8 minutes. There is a warm up exercise for 10 minutes. They dance for 35 minutes and then have a 15 minute cool down session. What time does the dance lesson finish? Give your answer using the 24-hour clock.

Answer [   ]

Question 8

School lessons start at 08.45am. They have two lessons before break time. Each lesson is 45 minutes long. What time will break time start?

Answer [   ]

Question 9

Lunch time starts at 12.50am. They have 50 minutes for lunch. Each lesson is 40 minutes long. How many lessons do they have left if their school day finishes at 15.00pm?

Answer [   ]

Question 10

A Geography lesson begins at 10.50am. They spend 10 minutes discussing the exercise, 30 minutes collecting data outside in the countryside, and 25 minutes writing up what they have have found. What time does the lesson finish?

Answer [   ]

Question 11

The school is taking part in a fun run. It consists of a 15 minute warm up, 5 minutes of preparation, and a 15 minute cooling down period. The run should take approximatley 38 minutes. If the race starts at 13.50pm, what time should the fun run finish? Give your answer using the 24-hour clock.

Answer [   ]

Question 12

A GCSE examination begins at 09.00am. They have 10 minutes planning time. They have 3 sections to complete each of which should take 25 minutes to complete. 5 minutes should remain to reread over their work. What time does the examination finish?

Answer [   ]

Question 13

A charity event hosted by the local school is taking place. There are 6 events taking place throughout the day. Each event should take approximatley 40 minutes. The charity event starts at 11.40am. What time should the charity event finish? Give your answer using the 24 – hour clock.

Answer

Question 14

On Fridays at the local school, they hold an assembly for all the pupils and staff. It takes 5 minutes to enter the hall, 10 minutes of the head teacher talking about important school issues, 12 minutes of hymns and 8 minutes of handing out awards and points for the school teams. The assembly starts at 9.10am. What time does the assembly finish?

Answer

Question 15

A History lesson begins at 11.40am. They spend 15 minutes discussing the history of WW2, 20 minutes discussing relevance and importance and 20 minutes creating a timeline to hang up on the classroom wall. They have 5 minutes to spare to start their homework before the end of the lesson. What time does the lesson finish?

Answer

Question 16

Pupils have 90 minutes to the end of the day. They have 2 lessons of 45 minutes. Their school day finishes at 15.15pm. What time is it? Give your answer using the 24 – hour clock.

Answer

Question 17

A French lesson begins at 11.50am. The teacher introduces the topic for 8 minutes, there is a warm up exercise for 12 minutes and the final task is completed in the last 40 minutes. When does the lesson end?

Answer

Question 18

It's sports day at a local school. It starts at 10.30am. In total, sports day is 300 minutes long. What time does sports day finish? Give your answer using the 24-hour clock.

Answer

Question 19

A History lesson begins at 09.10am. They spend 15 minutes discussing the history of World War One. They spend 10 minutes planning on how they are going to display all the information and then 40 minutes working on their presentations. What time does the lesson finish?

Answer

Question 20

Lessons begin at 08.45am. Each lesson is 45 minutes long. They have 2 lessons in between their break and lunch time. Break time starts at 10.40am. What time does lunch time start?

Answer

Question 21

The school is taking part in a cross country run. It consists of a 10 minute warm up and a 15 minute cooling down period. The run should take approximatley 48 minutes. The race starts at 12.40am. What time will the race finish? Give your answer using the 24-hour clock.

Answer

Question 22

An English Literature lesson starts at 09.30am. They are reading a play by Shakespeare. They spend 5 minutes deciding their roles, 33 minutes reading, and the last 12 minutes discussing what they have found. What time does the lesson finish?

Answer

Question 23

A-level exams are taking place. An Art exam has 3 sections, each of which are 50 minutes long. The exam begins at 09.00am. What time does the exam finish?

Answer

Question 24

A GCSE P.E lesson starts at 09.45am. There is 2 parts to the class – practical and theory. The practical consists of a warm up for 10 minutes, a cool down for 15 minutes and 40 minutes playing. The theory starts straight after the practical which lasts for 25 minutes. What time does the lesson finish?

Answer

Question 25

A Science class is taking part in a science fair. They have 10 minutes to plan and prepare, 8 minutes for discussion and 3 minutes to answer any questions. They will be penalised if they go over the time limit. If they begin their presentations at 10.45am, what time should their presentation be finished?

Answer [   ]

Now check your answers before moving onto the next section of the guide.

ANSWERS TO QTS NUMERACY TEST SECTION 5

1. 12.40pm

2. 10.57am

3. 12.50am

4. 65 minutes

5. 11.20am

6. 16 minutes

7. 11.58am

8. 10.15am

9. 2

10. 11.55am

11. 15.03pm

12. 10.30am

13. 15.40pm

14. 09.45am

15. 12.40am

16. 13.45pm

17. 12.50am

18. 15.30pm

19. 10.15am

20. 12.10am

21. 13.53pm

22. 10.20am

23. 11.30am

24. 11.15am

25. 11.06am

QTS NUMERACY TEST
SECTION 6

There are 25 questions in this sample test section and you have 12 minutes to complete them. You should be aiming to achieve a minimum of 16 correct answers from the 25 questions that are available.

QTS NUMERACY TEST SECTION 6

Question 1

A school calculates that it will give merits to boys and girls in the ratio of 4:1. There are a total of 680 merits given. How many merits do the girls get?

Answer

Question 2

There are 8 green balls and 4 red balls. What is the ratio of red balls to green balls? Give your answer in its simplest form.

Answer

Question 3

A class of 32 students has 12 boys. What is the ratio of boys to girls? Give your answer in its simplest form.

Answer

Question 4

Elliott and David are both runners at their school. Elliott can run a mile in 5 minutes and 50 seconds. David can run a mile in 6 minutes and 40 seconds. What is the ratio of Elliott's time to David's time? Give your answer in its simplest form.

Answer

Question 5

A school calculated how many golden stars were given to girls and boys in the ratio of 1:4. In the school year, a total of 780 merits were given out. How many merits did the boys get?

Answer [   ]

Question 6

A school has a total of 360 students. The ratio of girls to boys is 1:4. How many boys are there?

Answer [   ]

Question 7

A school choir has a total of 48 pupils with only 12 boys. What is the ratio of boys to girls? Give your answer in its simplest form.

Answer [   ]

Question 8

On a school trip, there are 48 students and 12 members of staff. What is the ratio of students to staff? Give your answer in its simplest form.

Answer [   ]

Question 9

In a school, grades in a Maths class showed that 1 out of 3 pupils were failing to achieve the average marks. The class consists of 36 pupils. How many pupils were achieving the average marks?

Answer [   ]

Question 10

A field trip to a stream by the local school required staff to students at the ratio of 1:3. There were 48 pupils attending the field trip. How many staff would be needed?

Answer [   ]

Question 11

A school has a total of 480 students. 320 of the students are girls. What is the ratio of girls to boys? Give your answer in its simplest form.

Answer [   ]

Question 12

A school dance has a total of 120 pupils attending. 70 of them are boys. What is the ratio of boys to girls? Give your answer in its simplest form.

Answer [   ]

Question 13

A school calculated that achievement awards were given to girls and boys in the ratio of 5:1. In the school year, a total of 840 achievement awards were given out. How many merits did the girls get?

Answer [   ]

Question 14

Mia and Beth are in the athletics club which they attend every other night after school. Mia can run 800m in 3 minutes. Beth can run 800m in 2 minutes 20 seconds. What is the ratio of Mia's time to Beth's time? Give your answer in its simplest form.

Answer [   ]

Question 15

In a junior school, there are 420 pupils. The number of students that have hot dinners instead of packed lunches is 4:1. How many students have hot dinners?

Answer [   ]

Question 16

240 students are taking their GCSE Maths exam. There are 90 girls in the examination. What is the ratio of girls to boys? Give your answer in its simplest form.

Answer [   ]

Question 17

In a school, the ratio of male to female staff is 1:3. If there are 15 female members of staff, how many male staff are there?

Answer [   ]

Question 18

A Food Technology class is making pastries. A recipe has flour, butter and water in the ratio of 12:8:4. If they used 3 cups of flour, how many cups of butter would be needed?

Answer [   ]

Question 19

A school disco has a total of 135 pupils attending. 65 of them are boys. What is the ratio of boys to girls? Give your answer in its simplest form.

Answer [   ]

Question 20

A school bake sale is taking place. 1:3 waiters for the event are girls. There are 28 waiters in total. How many boys are waiters for the event?

Answer [   ]

Question 21

A school has a total of 420 students. There are 160 girls. What is the ratio of girls to boys in the school? Give your answer in its simplest form.

Answer [   ]

Question 22

A teacher is off sick. Two classes have to merge together for the afternoon. The ratios of the English higher to English lower class are 1:3. In total, there are 64 pupils. How many pupils are from the higher English class?

Answer

Question 23

A school holds a talent contest. The ratio of boys to girls that enter is 5:2. 56 pupils enter the talent contest. How many pupils that enter the contest are boys?

Answer

Question 24

A field trip to a river requires staff to students in the ratio of 1:4. There are 65 pupils attending the field trip. How many staff would be needed?

Answer

Question 25

On a school trip, there are 56 pupils. 32 of which are girls. What is the ratio of girls to boys on the school trip?

Answer

Now check your answers before moving onto the next section of the guide.

ANSWERS TO QTS NUMERACY TEST SECTION 6

1. 136

2. 1:2

3. 3:5

4. 7:8

5. 624

6. 288

7. 1:3

8. 4:1

9. 27

10. 16

11. 2:1

12. 7:5

13. 700

14. 9:7

15. 336

16. 3:5

17. 5

18. 2

19. 13:14

20. 21

21. 8:13

22. 16

23. 40

24. 17

25. 4:3

QTS NUMERACY TEST
SECTION 7

There are 25 questions in this sample test section and you have 12 minutes to complete them. You should be aiming to achieve a minimum of 16 correct answers from the 25 questions that are available.

QTS NUMERACY TEST SECTION 7

Question 1

In a Junior School there are 240 pupils and 35% have free school dinners. Work out the number of children who do not have free school dinners.

Answer [   ]

Question 2

A local school has a total of 480 students. 55% of them are boys. Work out how many girls there are in the school.

Answer [   ]

Question 3

A secondary school has 40 members of staff. 25% of the staff work on a part time basis. How many staff work part time?

Answer [   ]

Question 4

A school has 460 students. They are allowed to accept another 20% of students, based on the total number of students they already have. How many more students are they allowed to accept?

Answer [   ]

Question 5

At a school, it has a total of 440 pupils. 35% of them get help with the cost of their school uniforms. How many pupils do not get help with their school uniform costs?

Answer [   ]

Question 6

There are a total of 520 pupils at a secondary school. 55% of them come from working class families. How many pupils come from working class families?

Answer [   ]

Question 7

40 pupils take part in a Maths challenge. 35% of them get knocked out by round 2. How many pupils are still left in the challenge?

Answer [   ]

Question 8

120 students take part in sports day. 60% of them are boys. Work out how many girls take part in sports day.

Answer [   ]

Question 9

120 is 20% of what?

Answer [   ]

Question 10

50 is 40% of what?

Answer [   ]

Question 11

A student scored 51/60 in their test. What is their test score as a %?

Answer [   ]

Question 12

School dinner fees go up by 8%. The monthly cost of school dinners is £46. What is the new price of school dinner fees each month?

Answer [   ]

Question 13

A student scores 67/80 on a Maths quiz. What is the percentage he scored on his Maths quiz?

Answer [   ]

Question 14

75 is 60% of what?

Answer [ ]

Question 15

In a Maths class there are 30 pupils. 10% of pupils are off with sickness. How many pupils are left in the class?

Answer [ ]

Question 16

25% of an English class received letters home concerning their grades. The English class has 48 pupils. How many pupils received letters home?

Answer [ ]

Question 17

A school has a total of 360 students. Over the year, 35% of pupils have been put on a school report regarding their behaviour at school. How many students have not been put on a school report?

Answer [ ]

Question 18

A secondary school has 48 members of staff. 25% of the staff work as a sub. How many staff work as a sub?

Answer [ ]

Question 19

A school has a total of 520 students. 60% of them are boys. Work out how many girls there are in the school.

Answer [   ]

Question 20

In a Maths class there are 40 pupils. 15% of pupils are sent out of the class to help set up the assembly hall. How many pupils are left in the class?

Answer [   ]

Question 21

A student scores 83/90 in a French test. What is the percentage he scored on his French test? Rounded to the nearest whole number.

Answer [   ]

Question 22

There are 360 pupils at a secondary school. 45% of pupils chose hot dinners over packed lunches. How many pupils chose packed lunches?

Answer [   ]

Question 23

52 pupils take part in a skills challenge. 25% of them get through to the semi-final. How many pupils managed to get to the semi-final of the skills challenge?

Answer [   ]

Question 24

A class of 32 receive their marks for their GCSE English exam. 75% of them received a grade between A-C. How many students received an A-C grade in their GCSE English exam?

Answer [   ]

Question 25

A local school has a total of 360 students. There are 180 boys. Work out the percentage of boys.

Answer [   ]

Now check your answers before moving onto the next section of your guide.

ANSWERS TO QTS NUMERACY TEST SECTION 7

1. 156

2. 216

3. 10

4. 92

5. 286

6. 286

7. 26

8. 48

9. 600

10. 125

11. 85%

12. £49.68

13. 83.75%

14. 125

15. 27

16. 12

17. 234

18. 12

19. 208

20. 34

21. 92%

22. 198

23. 13

24. 24

25. 50%

QTS NUMERACY TEST
SECTION 8

There are 25 questions in this sample test section and you have 12 minutes to complete them. You should be aiming to achieve a minimum of 16 correct answers from the 25 questions that are available.

QTS NUMERACY TEST SECTION 8

Question 1

220 pupils sit a GCSE Maths exam. The fraction of pupils who get Grade C or above is 3/5. How many pupils get Grade D or below?

Answer

Question 2

A student is given £15 lunch money for the week. He spends 2/5 of his money on energy drinks on the way home from school. How much money does he spend on energy drinks?

Answer

Question 3

Emma has a box of 15 chocolates that she is going to share with her friends at school. 10 are milk chocolate. What fraction of the whole box of chocolates is this?

Answer

Question 4

A junior school has 420 pupils. 3/5 of them receive free hot school dinners. What fraction of them do not receive free hot school dinners?

Answer

Question 5

In a school of 320 pupils, 2/5 of them receive cooked meals at school. How many pupils receive cooked meals when they go to school?

Answer

Question 6

Lucy has a bag of 6 counters to help her in her Maths lesson. 5 of them are red. The rest are blue. What fraction of the counters are blue?

Answer

Question 7

Its playtime and Jack gets out his sweets he bought from the shop this morning. He has twelve sweets. He gives a quarter of them to his friend Tony. How many sweets does he give away?

Answer

Question 8

19 fifths is an improper fraction. What mixed fraction is equal to this?

Answer

Question 9

8 thirds is an improper fraction. What mixed fraction is equal to this?

Answer

Question 10

There are 32 pupils in a Maths lesson. A quarter of them are off sick. How many pupils are in the Maths lesson?

Answer [   ]

Question 11

A Media lesson is split into thirds. 2/3 of the class are allowed out the classroom to film for their projects, the others must remain in the class until they come back. There are 42 students in the class. How many students have gone off filming?

Answer [   ]

Question 12

A school trip is taking place the following month. It costs each pupil £25 to go. However, the school needs to put down 2/3 of the money otherwise they lose their spot. 48 students are attending the school trip. How much money do the school need to put down?

Answer [   ]

Question 13

There are 42 members of staff working at a local secondary school. 3/7 of them are only part time workers. How many members of staff are only part time workers?

Answer [   ]

Question 14

A school assembly holds 120 pupils. They have calculated that 2/5 of the students will be receiving a golden star for their work ethic. How many students will not be receiving anything in the assembly?

Answer

Question 15

A student receives £35 a week for maintenance help. They decide to save ¾ of the money to put towards a holiday. How much money do they have to spend?

Answer

Question 16

3/7 of students are going to be put on a school report for their unacceptable behaviour. There are a total of 84 students in that year. How many students in that year will be going on a school report?

Answer

Question 17

During a school year, Lucy received 24 gold stars. 12 for excellent work, 6 for outstanding behaviour and 6 for great attendance. What fraction of Lucy's gold stars were for her outstanding behaviour? Write the fraction in its simplest form.

Answer

Question 18

9 fifths is an improper fraction. What mixed fraction is equal to this?

Answer [   ]

Question 19

7 thirds is an improper fraction. What mixed fraction is equal to this?

Answer [   ]

Question 20

A school has 360 pupils. 5/8 of them are in sports teams. How many pupils are not in a sports team?

Answer [   ]

Question 21

A total of 440 pupils attend a local secondary school. 1/8 of them are out sick for the day. How many pupils are at school that day if everyone else is to attend?

Answer [   ]

Question 22

It is teacher/parents day at a secondary school. For one student, it was calculated their feedback was good by ¾ of their teachers. They spoke to 8 teachers. How many teachers said good things about that pupil?

Answer [   ]

Question 23

8 thirds is an improper fraction. What mixed fraction is equal to this?

Answer [   ]

Question 24

7 quarters is an improper fraction. What mixed fraction is equal to this?

Answer [   ]

Question 25

A Film studies lesson is split into thirds. 1/3 of the class are allowed out the classroom at a given time to film for their presentations, the others must remain in the class until they come back. There are 36 students in the class. How many pupils remain in the classroom?

Answer [   ]

Now check your answers before moving onto the next section of the guide.

ANSWERS TO QTS NUMERACY TEST SECTION 8

1. 88

2. £6

3. 2/3

4. 2/5

5. 128

6. 1/6

7. 3

8. 3 4/5

9. 2 2/3

10. 24

11. 28

12. £800

13. 18

14. 72

15. £8.75

16. 36

17. 1/4

18. 1 4/5

19. 2 1/3

20. 135

21. 385

22. 6

23. 2 2/3

24. 1 3/4

25. 24

QTS NUMERACY TEST
SECTION 9

There are 25 questions in this sample test section and you have 12 minutes to complete them. You should be aiming to achieve a minimum of 16 correct answers from the 25 questions that are available.

QTS NUMERACY TEST SECTION 9

Question 1

A pupil scores 45.5% in Test 1 and 64.5% in Test 2. What was the pupil's average percentage score, assuming they were weighted equally?

Answer [   ]

Question 2

A student scores 68.5% on the first section of their exam and 72% on the second section of the exam. What was the student's average percentage score, assuming they were weighted equally?

Answer [   ]

Question 3

A pupil scores 48.5% in Test 1 and 69.5% in Test 2. What was the pupil's average percentage score, assuming they were weighted equally?

Answer [   ]

Question 4

A student scored 68.5% in Maths and 70.5% in Science. What was the student's average percentage score for both of those tests?

Answer [   ]

Question 5

A pupil scores 55% in English and 72.5% in English Literature. What was the pupil's average percentage score, assuming they were weighted equally?

Answer [   ]

Question 6

Calculate the average of these numbers. 46, 48 and 52. Round it up to the nearest whole number.

Answer [   ]

Question 7

Calculate the average of these numbers 47, 56 and 72. Round it up to the nearest whole number.

Answer [   ]

Question 8

The captain of the school cricket team is 19 years old. There are 11 other players on the team, 6 of which are 17, and 5 of them are 16. Work out the average age of all the players of the school cricket team.

Answer [   ]

Question 9

Mia and Rachel both received their marks back for their History exam. There were 2 sections in the test, so they received two marks. Mia scored 68% on the first section and 73% on the second. Rachel scored 74% on the first section and 64% on the second. Who scored the best average total?

Answer [   ]

Question 10

Two brothers go to the same school. One brother is 17 years old and the other is 15. They have twin sisters that go to another school. They are both 12. What is the average age of the brothers and sisters?

Answer [   ]

Question 11

Robert scored 82% in his theory in P.E and 93% in his practical. His friend Tom scored 84% in his theory and 89% in his practical. Work out both Robert's and Tom's average mark for P.E.

Answer

Question 12

Simon handed in 5 assignments for his English class over the academic year. His marks were as followed: 60, 63, 84, 73 and 87. Given that they are all equally weighted, what is Simon's average for English?

Answer

Question 13

A class of 12 in an A Level Maths lesson received their marks back for the test they done last week. 3 of them scored 74, 2 scored 54, 3 scored 71, 2 scored 85, 1 scored 55 and the other scored 68. Work out the average mark for the whole class. Round up to the nearest whole number.

Answer

Question 14

A student scores 83% on the first section of their exam and 79% on the second section of the exam. What was the student's average mark, assuming both sections were weighted equally?

Answer

Question 15

A student scores 92% in their written assessment. The written assessment is 40% of their total mark. They scored 87% in their examination which is worth 60%. What is the total average percentage score the student gets given that the written assessment is 40% and the exam is 60%?

Answer

Question 16

A student gets their marks back for their French GCSE. The oral part of the examination is worth 60%. The written assessment is worth 40%. The student scored 78% in the oral test and 84% in the written. What is the total average mark the student gets given the percentages of each part of the exam? Round up to the nearest whole number.

Answer

Question 17

Calculate the average of this set of data. 45, 83, 36, 85, 64, 74 and 52. Give your answer to the nearest whole number

Answer

Question 18

A class of 11 in an A Level English lesson received their marks back for the test they completed a few weeks back. Two of them scored 71, three scored 63, three scored 73, two scored 88 and one scored 49. Work out the average mark for the whole class. Round up to the nearest whole number.

Answer

Question 19

Cara scored 94% in her practical dance examination. She scored 89% in her written examination. The practical exam is worth 70% and the written exam is worth 30%. Work out Cara's average for her dance examination.

Answer [   ]

Question 20

Elliott got his marks back for his Geography exam. He got 5% for submitting his assignment in on time and handing in a plan. The first essay he scored 79 which is worth 40% and his second essay scored 84 which is worth 55%. Work out the total average of Elliott's Geography exam. Round it up to the nearest whole number.

Answer [   ]

Question 21

Calculate the average of this set of data: 65, 74, 56, 36, 95 and 56. Round it up to the nearest whole number.

Answer [   ]

Question 22

A pupil scores 89% in English and 73% in English Literature. What was the pupil's average percentage score, assuming they were weighted equally?

Answer [   ]

Question 23

A student scores 78% on part A of the exam and 84% on part B of the exam. What was the student's average percentage score, assuming both sections were weighted equally?

Answer [   ]

Question 24

A pupil scores 55% in Test 1 and 69% in Test 2. What was the pupil's average mark, assuming Test 1 is worth 60% and Test 2 is worth 40%? Round up to the nearest whole number.

Answer [   ]

Question 25

A student scores 75% on the first section of their exam and 92% on the second section of the exam. What was the student's average percentage score, assuming both sections were weighted equally?

Answer [   ]

Now check your answers before moving onto the next section of the guide.

ANSWERS TO QTS NUMERACY TEST SECTION 9

1. 55%

2. 70.25%

3. 59%

4. 69.5%

5. 63.75%

6. 49

7. 58

8. 16.75

9. Mia

10. 14

11. Robert = 87.5% Tom = 86.5%

12. 73.4

13. 70

14. 81%

15. 89%

16. 80%

17. 63

18. 70

19. 92.5%

20. 83%

21. 64

22. 81%

23. 81%

24. 61%

25. 83.5%

QTS NUMERACY TEST
SECTION 10

There are 25 questions in this sample test section and you have 12 minutes to complete them. You should be aiming to achieve a minimum of 16 correct answers from the 25 questions that are available.

QTS NUMERACY TEST SECTION 10

Question 1

There are 11 girls and 14 boys in a class. What is the percentage of girls in this class?

Answer [   ]

Question 2

There are 32 students in a class. 16 of them are boys. Work out the percentage of the number of girls in the class.

Answer [   ]

Question 3

There are 40 pupils in a class. There are 22 boys and 18 girls. Work out the percentage of the number of boys in the class.

Answer [   ]

Question 4

In a class there are 8 girls and 12 boys. What is the percentage of boys in this class?

Answer [   ]

Question 5

There are 36 members of staff at a primary school. 12 members of staff only work on a part time basis. What is the percentage of part time staff? Round up to the nearest whole number.

Answer [   ]

Question 6

In the lunch time hall, there are 120 students. 85 of them have hot school dinners. What is the percentage of students that do not have hot school dinners? To the nearest whole number.

Answer [   ]

Question 7

On a school trip there are 40 students and 15 members of staff. What is the total percentage of members of staff on the school trip?

Round up to the nearest whole number.

Answer [   ]

Question 8

Two classes are put together in the morning. Each class has 25 pupils. One class has 7 pupils that are vegetarian. The other class has 5 people that are vegetarian. In total, what is the total percentage of number of pupils that are vegetarian?

Answer [   ]

Question 9

A class of 24 has 12 pupils with blonde hair, 10 with brown and 2 with red hair. What is the percentage of number of pupils with brown hair? Round it up to the nearest whole number.

Round up to the nearest whole number.

Answer [   ]

Question 10

There are 46 members of staff. 8 of them have handed in their resignation. What is the percentage of number of staff members that have resigned?

Round up to the nearest whole number.

Answer

Question 11

In Year Five, there are 95 pupils. 18 of them are in the school choir. What is the percentage of the number of pupils that are not in the school choir?

Answer

Question 12

A local secondary school has a total of 340 students. 48 students have entered the local talent contest to represent their school. What is the percentage of the number of pupils that are representing their school?

Answer

Question 13

A school bake sale is taking place. 48 students got involved from Year six. There are a total of 105 students in that year. Work out the percentage of the number of pupils who did not take part in the school bake sale.

Answer

Question 14

In a local secondary school, there are a total of 520 students. 380 of them are in a team for their school. What is the percentage of number of people who are in a school team?

Answer [   ]

Question 15

In a class of 38 students, 26 of them come from working class families. What is the percentage of number of students that come from working class families?

Answer [   ]

Question 16

There are 160 students in Year Seven. There are 95 boys. Work out the percentage of the number of girls Year Seven. Round up to the nearest whole number.

Answer [   ]

Question 17

There are 32 students in a class. 11 of the students have allergies which are on school records. What is the percentage of number of students who do not have allergies in that class? Round up to the nearest whole number.

Answer [   ]

Question 18

Year Six has 125 pupils. 34 pupils this year have been put on a school report to monitor their attendance. What is the percentage of the number of pupils who are not on school reports? Round up to the nearest whole number.

Answer

Question 19

58 students are attending a field trip. There are 17 members of staff supervising the field trip. In total, what is the percentage of the number of staff attending the trip? Round up to the nearest whole number.

Answer

Question 20

There are 42 pupils in a class. There are 27 boys. Work out the percentage of the number of girls in the class. Round up to the nearest whole number.

Answer

Question 21

In the school dining hall, there are 168 pupils. 94 of them brought packed lunches. Work out the percentage of the number of pupils that have packed lunches. Round up to the nearest whole number.

Answer

Question 22

There are 38 members of staff at a primary school. 16 members of staff only work on a part time basis. What is the percentage of staff who are not part time?

Round up to the nearest whole number.

Answer [   ]

Question 23

A local school has 38 members of staff. They have employed another 6. What is the percentage increase of additional staff? Round up to the nearest whole number.

Answer [   ]

Question 24

A secondary school has a total of 280 students. 84 students have entered the cross country run around their town. What is the percentage of the number of students taking part in the cross country run?

Answer [   ]

Question 25

Year 5 are taking part in a healthy diet challenge. There are 38 pupils in the class. 21 pupils went home and got consent from their parents to take part, the other pupils' parents did not consent. What is the percentage of the number of pupils whose parents did not give them consent to take part in the healthy diet challenge? Round up to the nearest whole number.

Answer [   ]

Now check your answers before moving onto the next section of the guide.

ANSWERS TO QTS NUMERACY TEST SECTION 10

1. 44%

2. 50%

3. 55%

4. 60%

5. 33%

6. 29%

7. 27%

8. 24%

9. 42%

10. 17%

11. 81%

12. 14%

13. 54%

14. 73%

15. 68%

16. 41%

17. 66%

18. 73%

19. 23%

20. 36%

21. 56%

22. 58%

23. 16%

24. 30%

25. 45%

QTS NUMERACY TEST
SECTION 11

There are 25 questions in this sample test section and you have 12 minutes to complete them. You should be aiming to achieve a minimum of 16 correct answers from the 25 questions that are available.

QTS NUMERACY TEST SECTION 11

Question 1

A primary school has 80 pupils in year three. 10 pupils have a reading age that is below their actual age. Work out the percentage and then convert the number of pupils who have a reading age below their actual age, into a decimal.

Answer [   ]

Question 2

What is 30% as a decimal?

Answer [   ]

Question 3

What is 75% as a decimal?

Answer [   ]

Question 4

What is 23% as a decimal?

Answer [   ]

Question 5

What is 19.8% as a decimal?

Answer [   ]

Question 6

What is ½ as a decimal?

Answer [   ]

Question 7

What is 1/3 as a decimal?

Answer [   ]

Question 8

What is ¼ as a decimal?

Answer [   ]

Question 9

What is ¾ as decimal?

Answer [   ]

Question 10

What is 10% as a decimal?

Answer [   ]

Question 11

What is 1% as a decimal?

Answer [   ]

Question 12

What is 4/5 as a decimal?

Answer [   ]

Question 13

What is 92% as a decimal?

Answer [   ]

Question 14

What is 100% as a decimal?

Answer [   ]

Question 15

What is 5.6 as a percentage?

Answer [   ]

Question 16

What is 1/5 as a percentage?

Answer [   ]

Question 17

What is 85.5 as a percentage?

Answer [   ]

Question 18

Convert 13% into a decimal.

Answer [   ]

Question 19

Convert 1/6 as a decimal.

Answer [   ]

Question 20

What is 11.6 as a percentage?

Answer [   ]

Question 21

What is 66% as a decimal?

Answer [   ]

Question 22

What is 0.25 as a percentage?

Answer [   ]

Question 23

What is ¼ as a percentage?

Answer [   ]

Question 24

What is 0.145 as a percentage?

Answer [   ]

Question 25

What is 0.345 as a percentage?

Answer [   ]

Now check your answers before moving onto the next section of the guide.

ANSWERS TO QTS NUMERACY TEST SECTION 11

1. 0.125

2. 0.3

3. 0.75

4. 0.23

5. 0.198

6. 0.5

7. 0.333…

8. 0.25

9. 0.75

10. 0.1

11. 0.01

12. 0.8

13. 0.92

14. 1

15. 560%

16. 20%

17. 8550%

18. 0.13

19. 0.166…

20. 1160%

21. 0.66

22. 25%

23. 25%

24. 14.499%

25. 34.5%

QTS NUMERACY TEST
SECTION 12

There are 25 questions in this sample test section and you have 12 minutes to complete them. You should be aiming to achieve a minimum of 16 correct answers from the 25 questions that are available.

QTS NUMERACY TEST SECTION 12

Question 1

Two Geography classes get together to watch a video. The first class has 10 boys and 16 girls. The second class has 15 girls and 9 boys. When the class is combined what is the percentage of girls as a proportion of the total number of pupils?

Answer

Question 2

Two English classes are put together to role play a scene from Shakespeare's Romeo and Juliet. The first class has 14 girls and 18 boys. The second class has 15 girls and 19 boys. When the class is combined, what is the percentage of boys as a proportion of the total number of pupils? To the nearest whole number.

Answer

Question 3

In year six, there are 3 classes in which the pupils are divided into. The first class has 24 girls and 26 boys. The second class has 21 girls and 19 boys. The third class has 22 girls and 23 boys. If all of year six were combined, what is the percentage number of girls? Round up to the nearest whole number.

Answer

Question 4

A secondary school has a total of 450 students. 120 students have entered the cross country run around their town. 85 students that have entered are girls. What is the percentage of the number of girls taking part in the cross country run? Round up to the nearest whole number.

Answer

Question 5

Two Science classes come together to watch a scientist demonstrate a few experiments. The first class has 16 girls and 18 boys. The second class has 14 girls and 21 boys. When the class is combined, what is the percentage of girls as a proportion of the total number of pupils watching the science experiment? To the nearest whole number.

Answer [   ]

Question 6

Two History classes are invited on a school trip to the London Museum. Both classes have 38 students. The first class has 25 girls. The second class has 21 girls. When the classes are combined, what is the percentage of the number of boys attending the school trip? Round up to the nearest whole number.

Answer [   ]

Question 7

Two schools are competing in a football tournament. There are 145 pupils competing for one school and 152 pupils competing in the other. 60 girls from school one will be competing against the 72 girls from school two. In total, what is the percentage of the number of girls competing in the football tournament? To the nearest whole number.

Answer [   ]

Question 8

A field trip to an Art exhibition is happening for 3 of the GCSE Art classes. Each class has 25 students. The first class has 15 girls. The second class has 16 girls. The third class has 17 boys. If you combine all the Art classes, what is the percentage of the number of boys attending the Art exhibition?

Answer [   ]

Question 9

A teacher is off sick, so the school decides to combine all the English classes. The first class has 34 students. The second class has 29 students. Both classes have 18 boys. What is the percentage of the number of boys in the class when the class is combined?

Round up to the nearest whole number.

Answer [   ]

Question 10

A school has 42 employees. 31 of the employees are female. The school takes on 4 new members of staff, all of which are female. Work out the percentage of all the female staff. To the nearest whole number.

Answer [   ]

Question 11

32 parents help out on a school trip. 19 parents are male. Work out the percentage of female parents who attended the school trip. Round up to the nearest whole number.

Answer [   ]

Question 12

Sports day is taking place at a local secondary school. It's the parent's race and in total there are 56 parents who take part. 38 of the parents are female. What is the percentage of the number of male parents who took part in the race? To the nearest whole number.

Answer [   ]

Question 13

Two schools are competing in a tennis tournament. There are 98 pupils competing for one school and 103 pupils competing for the other. 39 girls from school one will be competing against the 44 girls from school two. In total, what is the percentage of the number of girls competing in the tennis tournament? To the nearest whole number.

Answer [   ]

Question 14

Two English classes are put together to role play a scene from Shakespeare's A Midsummer Night's Dream. The first class has 12 girls and 17 boys. The second class has 17 girls and 21 boys. When the classes are combined, what is the percentage of boys as a proportion of the total number of pupils? Round up to the nearest whole number.

Answer [   ]

Question 15

In a school choir, there are 42 pupils. 28 of the pupils are female. Work out the percentage of the number of males who are part of the school choir.

Answer [   ]

Question 16

In year seven, there are 3 classes in which the pupils are divided into. The first class has 21 girls and 26 boys. The second class has 19 girls and 24 boys. The third class has 22 girls and 18 boys. If all of year seven were combined, what is the percentage number of boys? To the nearest whole number.

Answer [   ]

Question 17

Two Food Technology classes come together to bake cakes for the school bake sale. The first class has 12 girls and 8 boys. The second class has 9 girls and 12 boys. When the classes are combined, what is the percentage of boys as a proportion of the total number of pupils baking for the school bake sale? Round up to the nearest whole number.

Answer

Question 18

A field trip to an Art gallery is happening for two of the GCSE Art classes. Each class has 21 students. The first class has 16 girls. The second class has 18 girls. If you combine the Art classes, what is the percentage of the number of girls attending the Art gallery? Round up to the nearest whole number.

Answer

Question 19

Two P.E classes are learning personal survival. Combining the classes, there is a total of 62 pupils. One class has 18 girls and the other class has 15 girls. What is the percentage of number of girls who attended the personal survival class? To the nearest whole number.

Answer

Question 20

A local secondary school has a total of 460 students. 108 students have entered the school talent contest. 73 of students who have entered are female. What is the percentage of the number of male pupils that have entered the school talent contest? To the nearest whole number.

Answer

Question 21

There are 160 students in Year Eight. There are 75 boys. Work out the percentage of the number of girls in Year Eight. To the nearest whole number.

Answer [   ]

Question 22

There are 34 students in a class. 12 of the students have been put on a school report regarding their behaviour. Out of the 12 students, 9 of these are boys. What is the percentage number of boys out of the total number of pupils who have been put on school report?

Answer [   ]

Question 23

58 students are attending a field trip. 32 students are male. What is the percentage number of female students attending the field trip? Round up to the nearest whole number.

Answer [   ]

Question 24

There are 40 pupils in a lower English class. There are 22 boys and 18 girls. The higher English class has 31 pupils. There is 13 boys and 18 girls. Work out the percentage of the number of boys if the English classes are combined. To the nearest whole number.

Answer [   ]

Question 25

There are 36 members of staff at a primary school. 22 members of staff are female. What is the percentage number of male staff that work at the primary school? Round up to the nearest whole number.

Answer [   ]

Now check your answers before moving onto the next section of the guide.

ANSWERS TO QTS NUMERACY TEST SECTION 12

1. 62%

2. 56%

3. 50%

4. 71%

5. 43%

6. 39%

7. 44%

8. 48%

9. 57%

10. 76%

11. 41%

12. 32%

13. 41%

14. 57%

15. 33%

16. 52%

17. 49%

18. 81%

19. 53%

20. 32%

21. 53%

22. 75%

23. 45%

24. 49%

25. 39%

QTS NUMERACY TEST
SECTION 13

There are 25 questions in this sample test section and you have 12 minutes to complete them. You should be aiming to achieve a minimum of 16 correct answers from the 25 questions that are available.

QTS NUMERACY TEST SECTION 13

Question 1

In a Science class 2/5 of the pupils achieved a level 5 in Key Stage 2. In another class ½ of the pupils achieve this level. What is the total fraction for both classes combined that achieves this level?

Answer [   ]

Question 2

In a Science class 2/5 of the pupils achieved level 5 in Key Stage 2. In another class ¼ of the pupils achieved this level. What is the total fraction for both classes combined that achieves this level?

Answer [   ]

Question 3

There are 2 tiers in Year Seven Maths – higher and lower. 3/8 of the higher level achieved a C grade. 1/4 of the lower level also achieved a C grade. What is the total fraction for both classes combined that achieved a C grade in Maths? In its simplest form.

Answer [   ]

Question 4

Two P.E classes are joined together. In one class, 1/6 of the pupils are female. In the other class, 5/12 of the pupils are female. Once combined, what is the total fraction for both classes that are female? In its simplest form.

Answer [   ]

Question 5

In an English exam, 1/8 achieved below their targeted grade. In a Science exam, 5/12 achieved below their targeted grade. What is the total fraction of both exams combined that achieved below their targeted grade?

Answer [   ]

Question 6

Two secondary schools compete in a football tournament. 2/9 of female pupils decide to play for the first school. 7/15 of female pupils decide to play for the second school. What is the total fraction of number of female pupils that take part in the football tournament?

Answer [   ]

Question 7

In a secondary school, 8/15 of staff members are male. In the primary school 3/10 of staff members are male. What is the total fraction of male staff members if you combine the secondary school and primary school? Give your answer in its simplest form.

Answer [   ]

Question 8

In Year six, there are 3 classes. In one class, 2/9 of pupils are female. In the second class, 5/12 of pupils are female. In the third class, 2/9 of pupils are female. What is the total fraction for all classes that are female?

Answer [   ]

Question 9

A school assembly is giving out golden awards for Year six. 3/10 of girls collect a gold award. ¼ of boys collect a gold award. What is the total fraction of students who collected a gold award from Year six? In its simplest form.

Answer [   ]

Question 10

For a Maths exam, 3/8 achieved the above and beyond award for great results. 4/12 in another Maths class achieved the above and beyond award. What is the total fraction of both exams combined that achieved the above and beyond award? In its simplest form.

Answer [   ]

Question 11

4/5 of an English class attended the History museum on a school trip. ¾ of a history class also attended the same trip. What is the total fraction of pupils who attended the history museum? Give your answer as a mixed fraction.

Answer [   ]

Question 12

Three classes are being monitored. 1/3 of the first class have seen an improvement in their science knowledge. 7/12 of the second class have also seen an improvement. 5/8 of the third class have also improved their knowledge in science. What is the total fraction of students that have improved their science knowledge across all three classes? Give your answer as a mixed fraction.

Answer [   ]

Question 13

Add up this set of data. 2/5, 3/10 and 8/15. Give your answer as a mixed fraction.

Answer [   ]

Question 14

Add up this set of data. 1/4, 2/8 and 3/12. Give your answer as a mixed fraction and in its simplest form.

Answer [   ]

Question 15

Teachers give out certificates for best behaviour and work in her class. 2/5 of girls collect a gold award. ¼ of boys collect a gold award. What is the total fraction of students who collected certificate from the class?

Answer [   ]

Question 16

There are 2 tiers in Year six English. 5/8 of the higher level achieved a C grade. 3/4 of the lower level also achieved a C grade. What is the total fraction for both classes combined that achieved a C grade in English? Give your answer as a mixed fraction. In its simplest form.

Answer [   ]

Question 17

3/5 of one GCSE P.E class are boys. The other GCSE P.E class is made up of ¼ of boys. What is the total fraction of boys in both GCSE P.E classes?

Answer [   ]

Question 18

1/5 of pupils in a class play a musical instrument. ½ of the class plays a sport. What is the total fraction of pupils who play a musical instrument and/or play a sport?

Answer [   ]

Question 19

3/8 of girls play football for the school team. 2/5 of boys play football for the school team. What is the total fraction of pupils who play football for the school team?

Answer [   ]

Question 20

A class studies how many pets they have. 1/8 of pupils have a hamster. 2/3 of pupils have a dog and 1/3 have a cat. What is the total fraction of pupils who have a hamster, dog and/or cat in the class? Give your answer as a mixed fraction. In its simplest form.

Answer [   ]

Question 21

2/4 of pupils in English received great feedback from their teachers on parent's day. 3/9 of pupils in Science received great feedback from their teachers. What is the total fraction of pupils who received great feedback from their teachers on parent's day? Give your answer in its simplest form.

Answer [   ]

Question 22

Two Science classes were doing Science experiments on the same day. Only some of the pupils from each class would be able to take part until the following week. 3/8 of one class took part in the Science experiment. ¼ of the other class took part in the Science experiment. What is the total fraction of pupils who took part in the Science experiment? In its simplest form.

Answer

Question 23

Add up this set of data of who has blonde hair across three English classes. ½ ¼ and 2/3. Give your answer as a mixed fraction.

Answer

Question 24

In a History class 3/5 of the pupils achieved level 4 in Key Stage 2. In another class 2/4 of the pupils achieved this level. What is the total fraction for both classes combined that achieves this level?

Answer

Question 25

Two dance classes are put together. In one class, 5/6 of the pupils are female. In the other class, 3/4 of the pupils are female. Once combined, what is the total fraction for both classes that are female? Give your answer as a mixed fraction. In its simplest form.

Answer

Now check your answers before moving onto the next section of the guide.

ANSWERS TO QTS NUMERACY TEST SECTION 13

1. 9/10

2. 13/20

3. 5/8

4. 7/12

5. 13/24

6. 31/45

7. 5/6

8. 31/36

9. 11/20

10. 17/24

11. 1 11/20

12. 1 13/24

13. 1 7/30

14. 3/4

15. 13/20

16. 1 3/8

17. 17/20

18. 7/10

19. 31/40

20. 1 1/8

21. 5/6

22. 5/8

23. 1 5/12

24. 1 1/10

25. 1 7/12

QTS NUMERACY TEST
SECTION 14

There are 25 questions in this sample test section and you have 12 minutes to complete them. You should be aiming to achieve a minimum of 16 correct answers from the 25 questions that are available.

QTS NUMERACY TEST SECTION 14

Question 1

A pupil scored 28%, 47% and 42% respectively in a three different maths tests. What was the pupil's mean percentage?

Answer [   ]

Question 2

A student scored 55% 63% and 71% in three different English tests. What was the student's mean percentage?

Answer [   ]

Question 3

A pupil scored 74% on Section A of the exam, 79% on Section B and 68% on Section C. What was the pupil's mean percentage? Round up to the nearest whole number.

Answer [   ]

Question 4

A school charges £3.20 for a hot school dinner. They charge £2.40 for cold school dinners. What is the mean price of buying a school dinner?

Answer [   ]

Question 5

Calculate the mean number of this set of data. 56 89 62 45

Answer [   ]

Question 6

Calculate the mean number of this set of data. 36 96 85 45 25

Answer [   ]

Question 7

Students work out the number of days in each month (assuming it's not a leap year). 7 months have 31 days. 4 months have 30 days. One month has 28 days. Calculate the mean number of days in a month. Round up to the nearest whole number.

Answer [   ]

Question 8

There are 21 staff at a primary school. 8 members receive the annual salary of £18,000. 9 members of staff receive £16,500. 4 members of staff receive £19,000. What is the mean salary of the primary school? Round up to the nearest whole number.

Answer [   ]

Question 9

Pupils from a school sell lemonade to raise money for charity. £122.50 is made by selling lemonade in a school week. What is the average daily amount the pupils make in a school week?

Answer [   ]

Question 10

A pupil took three Maths tests. They scored 76 marks in test 1, 65 marks in test 2 and 69 marks in test 3. What was the pupil's mean mark?

Answer [   ]

Question 11

A pupil had three exams for his Science GCSE. He scored 74% on exam 1, 86% on exam 2 and 65% on exam 3. What was the pupil's mean percentage for his science GCSE?

Answer [   ]

Question 12

Calculate the mean of this set of data. 79 85 61 38 65.

Answer [   ]

Question 13

Calculate the mean of this set of data. 132 198 206 197

Answer [   ]

Question 14

Each month the school receives donations from parents. 5 months they received £120. 4 months they received £95, 2 months they received £40 and one month they received £100. Work out the mean number of school donations given per month. Round up to the nearest whole number.

Answer [   ]

Question 15

A pupil scored 70% on Section A of the exam, 63% on Section B and 74% on Section C. What was the pupil's mean percentage?

Answer [   ]

Question 16

A pupil took four Geography tests in order to pass his GCSE. They scored 74 marks in test 1, 84 marks in test 2 and 59 marks in test 3 and 66 marks in test 4. What was the pupil's mean mark?

Answer [   ]

Question 17

8 pupils from a school took the 11 plus test to get into a grammar school. There marks were as followed. 69 52 49 71 63 70 70 69. What was the mean mark overall who took the 11 plus from that school?

Answer [   ]

Question 18

5 pupils had to retake their Maths exam. Their marks this time round were as followed. 69 59 86 75 68. What is the mean mark overall for the students who had to retake their maths exam?

Answer [   ]

Question 19

A teacher wanted to work out the mean mark for a student. She wanted to take into consideration her Maths, English and Science grades. Her grades were as followed. 79 65 56. What was the pupils mean mark if the teacher based the mark on these 3 grades? Round up to the nearest whole number.

Answer

Question 20

A pupil scored 86% on Section A of the exam and 91% on Section B What was the pupil's mean percentage?

Answer

Question 21

A pupil had three exams for his History GCSE. He scored 69% on exam 1, 82% on exam 2 and 83% on exam 3. What was the pupil's mean percentage for his history GCSE?

Answer

Question 22

Calculate the mean number of this set of data. 256 257 236 209 486

Answer

Question 23

Pupils from a school raise money each year for a charity of their choice. They raised in total £468 in 12 months. What is the mean average they raised per month?

Answer [   ]

Question 24

A student scored 79% 63% and 72% in three different Art exams. What was the student's mean percentage? Round up to the nearest whole number.

Answer [   ]

Question 25

A pupil scored 86% on Section A of the exam and 91% on Section B of their Maths exam. They scored 76% on Section A and 65% on Section B of their English exam. What was the pupil's mean percentage overall for both their Maths and English exams?

Answer [   ]

Now check your answers before moving onto the next section of the guide.

ANSWERS TO QTS NUMERACY TEST SECTION 14

1. 39%

2. 63%

3. 74%

4. £2.80

5. 63

6. 57.4

7. 30

8. £17,548

9. £24.50 a day

10. 70

11. 75%

12. 65.6

13. 183.25

14. £97

15. 69%

16. 70.75

17. 64.125

18. 71.4

19. 67

20. 88.5%

21. 78%

22. 288.8

23. £39

24. 71%

25. 79.5%

QTS NUMERACY TEST
SECTION 15

There are 25 questions in this sample test section and you have 12 minutes to complete them. You should be aiming to achieve a minimum of 16 correct answers from the 25 questions that are available.

QTS NUMERACY TEST SECTION 15

Question 1

What is 12.5% of 380 Kilograms?

Answer [   ]

Question 2

What is 25% of 260 kilograms?

Answer [   ]

Question 3

What is 60% of 580 pounds?

Answer [   ]

Question 4

What is 45% of 190 kilometres?

Answer [   ]

Question 5

What is 42% of 560 kilograms?

Answer [   ]

Question 6

What is 12.5% of 130 centimetres?

Answer [   ]

Question 7

What is 34.5% of 350 litres?

Answer [   ]

Question 8

What is 22.5% of 840 kilometres?

Answer [   ]

Question 9

What is 8.5% of 100 litres?

Answer [   ]

Question 10

What is 13.8% of 240 metres?

Answer [   ]

Question 11

What is 34.6% of 765?

Answer [   ]

Question 12

What is 57.2% of 400 gallons?

Answer [   ]

Question 13

What is 6.3% of 200 millilitres?

Answer [   ]

Question 14

What is 9.6% of 148 millimetres?

Answer [   ]

Question 15

What is 33.5% of 696 miles?

Answer [   ]

Question 16

What is 22% of 346?

Answer [   ]

Question 17

What is 88.5% of 1,000 metres?

Answer [   ]

Question 18

What is 62.3% of 480 litres?

Answer [   ]

Question 19

What is 1.8% of 10 millilitres?

Answer [   ]

Question 20

What is 21.45% of 500?

Answer [   ]

Question 21

What is 67% of 200?

Answer [   ]

Question 22

What is 15% of £15.60?

Answer [   ]

Question 23

What is 70% of £120?

Answer [   ]

Question 24

What is 61% of £578?

Answer [   ]

Question 25

What is 11.5% of £990?

Answer [   ]

Now check your answers before moving onto the next section of the guide.

ANSWERS TO QTS NUMERACY TEST SECTION 15

1. 47.5

2. 65

3. 348

4. 85.5

5. 235.2

6. 16.25

7. 120.75

8. 189

9. 8.5

10. 33.12

11. 264.69

12. 228.8

13. 12.6

14. 14.208

15. 233.16

16. 76.12

17. 885

18. 299.04

19. 0.18

20. 107.25

21. 134

22. £2.34

23. £84

24. £352.58

25. £113.85

QTS NUMERACY TEST
SECTION 16

There are 25 questions in this sample test section and you have 12 minutes to complete them. You should be aiming to achieve a minimum of 16 correct answers from the 25 questions that are available.

QTS NUMERACY TEST SECTION 16

Question 1

A school day ends at 3.30pm. In the afternoon there are only 2 sessions of 45 minutes with a 5 minute break in between. When does the afternoon sessions start? Give your answer using the 24 hour clock.

Answer [   ]

Question 2

A school day starts at 08.45am. In the morning there are only 2 lessons of 45 minutes before break time. What time does break time start?

Answer [   ]

Question 3

A school day ends at 3.15pm. In the afternoon there are only 2 lessons of 50 minutes long. When does the afternoon sessions begin? Give your answer using the 24-hour clock.

Answer [   ]

Question 4

Break time starts at 10:30am. It lasts for 20 minutes. There are 2 lessons of 45 minutes each before lunch time. What time does lunch time start?

Answer [   ]

Question 5

Teachers stay 90 minutes behind after school to begin marking. The school day finishes at 3.20pm. What time do the teachers leave? Give your answer using the 24-hour clock.

Answer

Question 6

The school day finishes at 3.00pm. Some students stay behind after school for homework club. Homework club lasts 70 minutes. What time do the students who stay behind leave school? Give your answer using the 24-hour clock.

Answer

Question 7

In a school day there are 6 lessons. Each lesson is 50 minutes long. There is a break for 30 minutes and lunch lasts for 60 minutes. If the school day starts at 8.45am, what time does the school day finish? Give your answer using the 24-hour clock.

Answer

Question 8

A school day ends at 1520pm. In the afternoon there are only 2 lessons of 45 minutes long. When does the afternoon sessions begin? Give your answer using the 24-hour clock.

Answer

Question 9

A school day starts at 08.45am. In the morning there are only 2 lessons of 50 minutes before break time. Break time lasts for 20 minutes. What time does break time finish?

Answer [   ]

Question 10

GCSE P.E have a practical session and then a theory session straight after. Their practical session lasts 70 minutes and their theory session lasts 50 minutes. If they begin their practical session at 11.45am, what time will they finish their practical session? Give your answer using the 24-hour clock.

Answer [   ]

Question 11

The school day starts at 0845am. They have 15 minutes form time and then a 25 minute assembly before lessons start. What time does lessons begin?

Answer [   ]

Question 12

Citizenship class starts at 0915am. Each lesson is 50 minutes long. A pupil is taken out of class at the beginning to get extra help in English. They are gone for 35 minutes. What time does the pupil arrive back in the citizenship class?

Answer [   ]

Question 13

Break time finishes at 10.30am. They have 3 lessons of 45 minutes each before lunch time. What time does lunch time start?

Answer [   ]

Question 14

It is sports day at the local primary school. 8 events are taking place, usually lasting 35 minutes. If sports day starts at 10.30am, what time will sports day finish, given that it takes the usual amount of time for completion? Give your answer using the 24-hour clock.

Answer [   ]

Question 15

A GCSE Science exam is taking place. It lasts for 90 minutes. A GCSE Art exam is taking place half an hour after the science exam finishes. The Art exam lasts for 120 minutes. A pupil has to sit both exams, which begins at 09.00am. What time will they finish both exams if everything runs on time? Give your answer using the 24-hour clock.

Answer [   ]

Question 16

A school trip is taking place at Dover Castle. They are leaving the school grounds at 09.30am. It takes an hour each way and they will be there for 3 and a half hours. What time should parents expect to pick up the children from school? Give your answer using the 24-hour clock.

Answer [   ]

Question 17

Break time starts at 10:15am. It lasts for 25 minutes. There are 2 lessons of 50 minutes each before lunch time. What time does lunch time start?

Answer

Question 18

A school day starts at 08.45am. In the morning there is a 15 minute form time, 2 lessons of 45 minutes and a break time that lasts 20 minutes. What time does break time finish?

Answer

Question 19

Teachers stay 110 minutes behind after school for a teacher's conference. The school day finishes at 1520pm. What time do the teachers leave? Give your answer using the 24-hour clock.

Answer

Question 20

A pupil gets home at 16.00pm. He has 3 sets of homework to do after dinner. Each piece of homework should take 25 minutes. He begins his homework at 17.50pm. What time will he finish his homework? Give your answer using the 24-hour clock.

Answer

Question 21

A school day starts at 08.30am. In the morning there are only 2 lessons of 45 minutes before break time. Break time lasts for 25 minutes. What time does the next section of the day start?

Answer [   ]

Question 22

Break time finishes at 10.35am. They have 3 lessons of 50 minutes each before lunch time. What time does lunch time start? Give your answer using the 24-hour clock.

Answer [   ]

Question 23

The school day starts at 08.45am. A pupil is running late by 100 minutes. What time will the pupil arrive at school?

Answer [   ]

Question 24

Break finishes at 10:45am. Until the end of the day, pupils have 4 more lessons of 50 minutes each plus an hour's lunch. What time does their school day end? Give your answer using the 24-hour clock.

Answer [   ]

Question 25

A school trip is taking place to London. They are leaving the school grounds at 09.15am. It takes 70 minutes each way and they will be there for 300 minutes. What time should parents expect to pick up the children from school? Give your answer using the 24-hour clock.

Answer [   ]

Now check your answers before moving onto the next section of the guide.

ANSWERS TO QTS NUMERACY TEST SECTION 16

1. 13:55

2. 10:15

3. 13:35

4. 12:20

5. 16.50

6. 16:10

7. 15:15

8. 13:50

9. 10:45

10. 13:45

11. 09:25

12. 09:50

13. 12:45

14. 15:10

15. 13:00

16. 15:00

17. 12:20

18. 10:50

19. 17:10

20. 19:05

21. 10:25

22. 13:05

23. 10:25

24. 15:05

25. 16:35

QTS NUMERACY TEST
SECTION 17

There are 25 questions in this sample test section and you have 12 minutes to complete them. You should be aiming to achieve a minimum of 16 correct answers from the 25 questions that are available.

QTS NUMERACY TEST SECTION 17

Question 1

A History class joins a Science class for a school trip. The total number of pupils in this trip is 49. If 3/7 of the pupils were from the Science class, how many pupils were there from the History class?

Answer [   ]

Question 2

A GCSE P.E class and an A Level P.E class join together. The total number of pupils in the class is 56. If 4/7 of the pupils were from the GCSE P.E class, how many pupils were there from the A Level P.E class?

Answer [   ]

Question 3

A teacher is off sick. Two English classes are joined together. In total there are 48 students. 3/8 of the students are boys. How many pupils in total are girls?

Answer [   ]

Question 4

Year eight received their GCSE results. In total, 132 pupils took their GCSE's. 8/12 of pupils received grades C or above. How many pupils received below a C grade?

Answer [   ]

Question 5

A secondary school has 3 school trips on the same day. In total there are 480 students who attend that secondary school. 3/8 of pupils are going on the school trip. How many students will not be going on a school trip?

Answer [   ]

Question 6

Two English classes are put together to act out a role play from a scene of Macbeth. There are 20 pupils in the first class and 30 pupils in the second. Work out the fraction of pupils who comes from the first class, in proportion to the total number of pupils. Provide answer in its simplest form.

Answer [   ]

Question 7

A secondary school takes part in a cross country run. In total, 147 pupils take part. 3/7 of the pupils are girls. How many pupils who took part in the cross country run were boys?

Answer [   ]

Question 8

Three Science classes take part in a science experiment. In total, there are 72 students taking part. 1/3 of the class are allowed to take part in the experiment at one time. How many students take part in a given time?

Answer [   ]

Question 9

Two History classes and an Art class go on a school trip to a London Museum. In total, there are 96 students. 4/6 of the students are there for History. How many students are there from the Art class?

Answer [   ]

Question 10

A football tournament is taking place at the local primary school. Two schools are attending. In total, there are 105 pupils taking part. 2/5 of pupils are from the other school. How many pupils are taking part from the local primary school?

Answer [   ]

Question 11

A secondary school has 48 employees. ¼ of them work on a part time basis. How many employees work on a part time basis?

Answer [   ]

Question 12

A school trip needs parents to help supervise the students. In total, 36 parents help out. 4/6 of them are female. How many parents that help out are male?

Answer [   ]

Question 13

It is sports day at a school. There are 224 students taking part in a sporting event. 4/7 of the students are male. What is the number of female pupils that are taking part in sports day?

Answer [ ]

Question 14

A school enters the local talent contest. From that school, 48 pupils audition. 1/3 of them get through to the next stage. How many pupils from that school get through to the next round?

Answer [ ]

Question 15

A school choir consists of 54 pupils. 2/3 of the choir are girls. Work out the number of pupils in the choir that are male.

Answer [ ]

Question 16

A school puts on a bake sale. They bake a total of 400 cakes/cookies. 2/5 of the total amount are cakes. How many cookies did they bake?

Answer [ ]

Question 17

In assembly, year eight are given golden stars. In total, 48 golden stars are given out. 4/6 of these golden stars are awarded to girls. How many golden stars are awarded to boys?

Answer [ ]

Question 18

A GCSE Media class consists of 45 pupils. 5/9 of the pupils achieved A-C grades in their last quiz. How many pupils did not receive an A-C grade?

Answer [   ]

Question 19

A primary school has a total of 32 teachers. 7/8 of the teachers are female. How many of the teachers working at the primary school are male?

Answer [   ]

Question 20

There are 424 pupils in a secondary school. 1/8 of pupils have been put on a school report to monitor their attendance. How many pupils have been put on a school report?

Answer [   ]

Question 21

A school trip to a London Theatre is taking place for two classes – performing arts dance and performing arts acting. In total, there are 88 students attending the trip. 3/8 of students are there for performing arts dance. How many pupils are there from the performing arts acting?

Answer [   ]

Question 22

Year twelve have received their A Level results. 140 pupils took their A Levels, and 3/7 of the pupils received A-C grades. How many pupils received below a C grade?

Answer [   ]

Question 23

A GCSE Film class consists of 27 pupils. 7/9 of the pupils achieved A-C grades in their last quiz. How many pupils did not receive an A-C grade?

Answer [   ]

Question 24

A school trip to Leeds Castle is taking place. 16 teachers are supervising as well as 8 parents. In total, there are 24 supervisors. 3/6 of supervisors are male. How many supervisors are female?

Answer [   ]

Question 25

Two GCSE dance classes join together. The total number of pupils in the class is 35. If 3/7 of the pupils were from one dance class, how many pupils were there from the second dance class?

Answer [   ]

Now check your answers before moving onto the next section of the guide.

ANSWERS TO QTS NUMERACY TEST SECTION 17

1. 28

2. 24

3. 30

4. 44

5. 300

6. 2/5

7. 84

8. 24

9. 32

10. 63

11. 12

12. 12

13. 96

14. 16

15. 18

16. 240

17. 16

18. 20

19. 4

20. 53

21. 55

22. 80

23. 6

24. 12

25. 20

QTS NUMERACY TEST
SECTION 18

There are 25 questions in this sample test section and you have 12 minutes to complete them. You should be aiming to achieve a minimum of 16 correct answers from the 25 questions that are available.

QTS NUMERACY TEST SECTION 18

Question 1

A coach can accommodate 54 people. There are 36 pupils who go on a school outing in this coach. During the outing there has to be one teacher for every 6 pupils. How many vacant seats are there?

Answer [   ]

Question 2

A school hall can accommodate 210 chairs. There are 48 students and 91 parents in a special awards ceremony. How many vacant seats are there?

Answer [   ]

Question 3

A school trip to Dover Castle is taking place. They have booked a coach that has 64 seats. There are 36 students attending the trip. During which, one teacher is needed to supervise 6 students. How many vacant seats are there?

Answer [   ]

Question 4

Two Science classes are joined together to work on a science experiment about the solar system. In total, there are 48 students. The teacher choses 6 captains, who then get to take it in turns and pick their teams. How many students do the captain's get to pick?

Answer [   ]

Question 5

A school trip to Thorpe Park is taking place. In total, there are 77 students. There are 13 supervisors who can supervise up to 6 children. With this in mind, how many groups will the students be divided into given that there are 13 supervisors?

Answer

Question 6

A school trip is taking place to a London Museum. They have booked two coaches which has 54 seats per coach. There are 75 students attending the trip. During which, one teacher is needed to supervise 5 students. How many vacant seats are there?

Answer

Question 7

The school is taking part in a school challenge. The challenge is taking place at a different venue so they are driving there. 32 students are taking part in the skills challenge. If all 8 cars are 5-seater, and has one adult driver, how many vacant seats will there be?

Answer

Question 8

Two English classes are role playing scenes from Romeo and Juliet. In total, there are 55 students. In each group, for every 2 boys there needs to be 3 girls. How many groups will be needed to accommodate all the students?

Answer

Question 9

A Geography class is going on a school trip to take notes on the country-side. A coach is needed to take them all there and back. The coach can accommodate 52 people. There are 41 pupils who are going on the trip. One teacher will be needed for every 7 students. How many vacant seats are there on the coach?

Answer [   ]

Question 10

A local primary school is putting on a Christmas show. In total, there are 180 chairs in the school hall. There are 63 pupils and 98 parents. 14 teachers also watch the show. How many vacant seats are there?

Answer [   ]

Question 11

A Science class is taking part in a science experiment. There are 32 students in a class. The safety procedures of this science experiment requires 1 supervisor for every 4 students. How many supervisors would be needed for this experiment?

Answer [   ]

Question 12

Two Media classes are filming for their final GCSE projects. In total, there are 49 students. The teacher splits the groups into 3 boys and 4 girls. How many groups in total did the teacher split the class in to in order to accommodate for all the students?

Answer [   ]

Question 13

A school trip is taking place to watch Les Miserables in a London Theatre. They have booked two coaches that have 64 seats. There are 84 students attending the trip. During which, one supervisor is needed to supervise 8 students. How many vacant seats are there?

Answer [   ]

Question 14

Two GCSE P.E classes are joined together to play tennis. In total, there are 48 students. They play in groups of 4. There is only 4 tennis courts to play on. How many students have to sit out whilst the others play at one given time?

Answer [   ]

Question 15

A skills challenge is taking place at a local secondary school. In total, 63 pupils take part. For every group, there is 3 boys to every 4 girls. How many groups would be needed to accommodate all 63 pupils?

Answer [   ]

Question 16

A school is taking a trip to France. There are 54 students attending the trip. During which, one teacher is needed to supervise 6 students. How many supervisors will be needed to accommodate all the students?

Answer [   ]

Question 17

Two History classes and an Art class are all going on the same trip to the British Museum. In total there are 86 pupils attending the trip. The school has booked two coaches that have 55 seats each. In order for the students to go on the trip, one supervisor is needed for every 8 pupils. How many vacant seats will there be on the coach?

Answer [   ]

Question 18

A football tournament is taking place at a local secondary school. In total, there are 108 pupils taking part. Each team has 12 members. There are 4 football pitches. How many teams can play at the same time?

Answer [   ]

Question 19

A GCSE Film class has a total of 32 pupils. Every 8 students are allowed to leave the classroom to go filming for their projects. How many times during the lesson do students leave the classroom in order to get their filming done?

Answer [   ]

Question 20

Two Geography classes and an Environmental Science class are all going on the same trip. In total there are 74 pupils attending the trip. The school has booked two coaches that has 56 seats each. In order for the students to go on the trip, one supervisor is needed for every 6 pupils. How many vacant seats will there be on the coach?

Answer [   ]

Question 21

Year eight received their GCSE results. In total, 91 pupils out of 120 who took their GCSE's received A-C grades. For every 3 girls who got A-C grades, 4 boys achieved A-C grades. How many boys achieved A-C grades?

Answer

Question 22

A school is taking a trip to Germany. There are 64 students attending the trip. During which, one teacher is needed to supervise 5 students. How many supervisors will be needed to accommodate all the students?

Answer

Question 23

A school dining hall can accommodate 175 chairs. There are 168 students and 7 supervisors who sit in the dining hall for lunch time. How many vacant seats are there?

Answer

Question 24

Two English classes and a History class are all going on the same trip. In total there are 66 pupils attending the trip. The school has booked two coaches that has 56 seats each. In order for the students to go on the trip, one supervisor is needed for every 5 pupils. How many vacant seats will there be on the coach?

Answer

Question 25

A secondary school has a school trip to Wales. They have booked a coach that has 52 seats. There are 41 students attending the trip. During which, one teacher is needed to supervise 5 students. How many vacant seats are there?

Answer [   ]

Now check your answers before moving onto the next section of the guide.

ANSWERS TO QTS NUMERACY TEST SECTION 18

1. 12

2. 71

3. 22

4. 7

5. 13

6. 18

7. None

8. 11

9. 5

10. 5

11. 8

12. 7

13. 33

14. 32

15. 9

16. 9

17. 13

18. 8

19. 4

20. 25

21. 52

22. 13

23. None

24. 32

25. 2

QTS NUMERACY TEST
SECTION 19

There are 25 questions in this sample test section and you have 12 minutes to complete them. You should be aiming to achieve a minimum of 16 correct answers from the 25 questions that are available.

QTS NUMERACY TEST SECTION 19

Question 1

A teacher needs to write reports in her subject for 32 pupils. Each report will take her an average of 9 minutes to write. She also spends an average of 4 minutes checking each report. How long in hours and minutes does it take the teacher to finish the entire report writing tasks?

Answer [   ]

Question 2

A teacher needs to mark 42 test papers. Each test takes approximately 9 minutes to mark. She also spends 3 minutes checking over each report. How long in hours and minutes will it take for the teacher to finish marking the test papers?

Answer [   ]

Question 3

A teacher gives out a Maths quiz in her GCSE Maths class. There are 29 pupils in her class. Each test takes about 6 minutes to mark, with 2 minutes to check over each test. How long in hours and minutes will it take for the teacher to finish marking the Maths quizzes?

Answer [   ]

Question 4

The English GCSE mock exam is taking place. There are 72 pupils taking the mock exam. Each test paper takes approximately 11 minutes to mark with 4 minutes for checking over each paper. How long in hours and minutes will it take overall to finish marking the mock papers?

Answer [   ]

Question 5

A student mentors two year 7 boys in English. In 2 weeks, the boys complete 3 quizzes each. It takes approximately 6 minutes to mark each quiz, with an added 2 minutes to check it over. How long in minutes does it take the mentor to mark the two boys' quizzes?

Answer

Question 6

A GCSE P.E class of 38 pupils take a practice exam. There are 2 sections. Each section takes approximately 7 minutes to mark. The teacher also spends 3 minutes at the end to check over the whole paper. How long in hours and minutes will it take the teacher to mark all the practice exam papers for her GCSE P.E class?

Answer

Question 7

A teacher gives out a pop quiz in her History class. There are 33 pupils in her class. She takes the quizzes home to mark. Each quiz takes approximately 5 minutes to mark with 2 minutes to check over her marking. How long in hours and minutes will it take the teacher to finish the marking of the pop quizzes?

Answer

Question 8

A mock Science exam needs to be marked for 52 pupils. The papers need to be marked by two different people. Each exam takes approximately 6 minutes to mark with 3 minutes to check over the whole exam. How long in hours and minutes does it take in total for the science exam papers to be marked by two markers?

Answer

Question 9

An English class of 28 have just sat a mock exam. The exam has 2 sections – literature and poetry. It takes approximately 6 minutes to mark the literature section and 7 minutes to mark the poetry section. Another 2 minutes is given on each exam to check the work again. How long in hours and minutes does it take to mark the English mock exam?

Answer [   ]

Question 10

A History class sits two History tests over the course of 2 days. The History class has 30 pupils. Each test takes approximately 8 minutes to mark with 3 minutes to go over the work again. How long in hours and minutes will it take the teacher to complete the marking for all the History tests?

Answer [   ]

Question 11

Pupils of a secondary school are taking their A Level English exam. The exam lasts for 150 minutes. How long in minutes and hours are the pupils sat taking their A Level English exam?

Answer [   ]

Question 12

A teacher needs to mark 41 test papers. Each test takes approximately 8 minutes to mark. She also spends 3 minutes checking over each report. How long in hours and minutes will it take for the teacher to finish marking the test papers?

Answer [   ]

Question 13

A teacher needs to mark 60 English test papers. Each test takes approximately 7 minutes to mark. She also spends 5 minutes checking over each report. How long in hours and minutes will it take for the teacher to finish marking the test papers?

Answer [   ]

Question 14

A Science and Maths GCSE exam are taking place on the same day. Each test takes about 11 minutes to mark and 3 minutes to check it over. 32 people sit the Science exam and 28 people sit the Maths exam. How long in hours and minutes will it take to mark both the GCSE Science and Maths exams?

Answer [   ]

Question 15

A teacher gives out a History quiz in her History class. There are 27 pupils in her class. Each test takes about 6 minutes to mark, with 3 minutes to check over each test. How long in hours and minutes will it take for the teacher to finish marking the History quizzes?

Answer [   ]

Question 16

A teacher needs to mark 47 test papers. Each test takes approximately 9 minutes to mark. She also spends 4 minutes checking over each report. How long in hours and minutes will it take for the teacher to finish marking the test papers?

Answer [   ]

Question 17

A student mentors four year seven pupils in English. The pupils complete 4 quizzes each. It takes approximately 8 minutes to mark each quiz, with an added 3 minutes per quiz to check over. How long in minutes does it take the mentor to mark all the quizzes?

Answer

Question 18

A teacher needs to write end of year reports for her 42 students. Each report takes approximately 13 minutes to write. The teacher also spends an average of 4 minutes checking the report. How long does it take in hours and minutes to finish the reports for her students?

Answer

Question 19

A teacher writes grade reports for her Science classes. She has three classes, a class of 32, a class of 27 and a class of 29. The teacher spends an average of 8 minutes writing the report and another 4 minutes checking it over. How long does it take in hours and minutes to finish writing the grade reports for all her classes?

Answer

Question 20

A Film class of 31 have just sat a mock Exam. The exam has 2 sections – a short screening and 2 essays. It takes approximately 14 minutes to mark each exam. They also spend 4 minutes checking over the whole exam. How long in hours and minutes does it take to mark the Film mock exam?

Answer

Question 21

A Geography class have taken a short test. The teacher spends 6 minutes marking and 2 minutes checking over the tests. There are 23 pupils in the Geography class. How long in hours and minutes does it take to mark the Geography tests?

Answer [   ]

Question 22

At a secondary school, they are having sports day. It starts at 09.30am and finishes at 15.15pm. How long in hours and minutes does sports day last for?

Answer [   ]

Question 23

A local primary school is putting on a Christmas play. It starts at 18.20pm and the play finishes at 20.10pm. How long in hours and minutes does the Christmas play last for?

Answer [   ]

Question 24

The school day starts at 08.30am and finishes at 15.15pm. The school day finishes at 15.15. How long in hours and minutes are students at school for?

Answer [   ]

Question 25

The Geography GCSE mock exam is taking place. There are 54 pupils taking the mock exam. Each test paper takes approximately 13 minutes to mark with 3 minutes for checking over each paper. How long in hours and minutes will it take overall to finish marking the mock papers?

Answer [   ]

Now check your answers before moving onto the next section of the guide.

ANSWERS TO QTS NUMERACY TEST SECTION 19

1. 6 hours and 56 minutes

2. 8 hours and 24 minutes

3. 3 hours and 52 minutes

4. 18 hours

5. 48 minutes

6. 10 hours and 46 minutes

7. 3 hours and 51 minutes

8. 15 hours and 36 minutes

9. 7 hours and 56 minutes

10. 11 hours

11. 2 hours and 30 minutes

12. 7 hours and 31 minutes

13. 12 hours

14. 14 hours

15. 4 hours and 3 minutes

16. 10 hours and 11 minutes

17. 2 hours and 56 minutes

18. 11 hours and 54 minutes

19. 17 hours and 36 minutes

20. 9 hours and 18 minutes

21. 3 hours and 4 minutes

22. 5 hours and 45 minutes

23. 1 hour and 50 minutes

24. 6 hours and 45 minutes

25. 14 hours and 24 minutes

QTS NUMERACY TEST
SECTION 20

There are 25 questions in this sample test section and you have 12 minutes to complete them. You should be aiming to achieve a minimum of 16 correct answers from the 25 questions that are available.

QTS NUMERACY TEST SECTION 20

Question 1

What is 454 divided by 0.2?

Answer

Question 2

What is 121 divided by 0.1?

Answer

Question 3

What is 254 divided by 0.1?

Answer

Question 4

What is 469 divided by 0.1?

Answer

Question 5

What is 383 divided by 0.2?

Answer

Question 6

What is 429 divided by 0.2?

Answer [   ]

Question 7

What is 846 divided by 0.3?

Answer [   ]

Question 8

What is 291 divided by 0.3?

Answer [   ]

Question 9

What is 843 divided by 0.6?

Answer [   ]

Question 10

What is 593 divided by 0.2?

Answer [   ]

Question 11

What is 733 divided by 0.1?

Answer [   ]

Question 12

What is 1232 divided by 0.1?

Answer

Question 13

What is 2468 divided by 0.2?

Answer

Question 14

What is 4863 divided by 0.3?

Answer

Question 15

What is 85 divided by 0.5?

Answer

Question 16

What is 96 divided by 0.8?

Answer

Question 17

What is 27 divided by 0.1?

Answer

Question 18

What is 265 divided by 0.5?

Answer

Question 19

What is 246 divided by 0.6?

Answer

Question 20

What is 621 divided by 0.3?

Answer

Question 21

What is 1346 divided by 0.1?

Answer

Question 22

What is 742 divided by 0.2?

Answer

Question 23

What is 985 divided by 0.5?

Answer

Question 24

What is 1234 divided by 0.4?

Answer [   ]

Question 25

What is 26 divided by 0.2?

Answer [   ]

Now check your answers before moving onto the next section of the guide.

ANSWERS TO QTS NUMERACY TEST SECTION 20

1. 2270

2. 1210

3. 2540

4. 4690

5. 1915

6. 2145

7. 2820

8. 970

9. 1405

10. 2965

11. 7330

12. 12320

13. 12340

14. 16210

15. 170

16. 120

17. 270

18. 530

19. 410

20. 2070

21. 13460

22. 3710

23. 1970

24. 3085

25. 130

QTS NUMERACY TEST
SECTION 21

There are 10 questions in this sample test section, and you have 8 minutes to complete them.

QTS NUMERACY TEST SECTION 21

Question 1

The lowest score on a Maths test is 53. The highest score is 92. The median score is 71. The lower quartile is 56 and the upper quartile is 87. Represent this information with a box-and-whisker plot.

Answer

Question 2

The lowest score on the year nine History test is 5 out of 20. The highest score was 19. The median score is 11. The lower quartile is 9 and the upper quartile is 15.

Represent this information with a box-and-whisker plot.

Answer

Question 3

The lowest score in the year seven Science tests was 65. The highest score was 95. The median score was 80. The lower quartile score was 70 and the upper quartile score was 85. Represent this information with a box-and-whisker plot.

Answer

Question 4

The lowest percentage for attendance in year seven was 51%. The highest attendance was 100%. The median percent for attendance is 70%. The lower quartile percent was 61% and the upper quartile percent was 90%.

Represent this information with a box-and-whisker plot.

Answer

Question 5

The lowest number of golden stars awarded for year seven is 0. The highest number is 20. The median number of golden stars is 11. The lower quartile number is 8 and the upper quartile number is 16. Represent this information with a box-and-whisker plot.

Answer

Question 6

The quickest time for the schools cross country team was 12 minutes. The slowest time for the team was 22 minutes. The median time was 16 minutes. The lower quartile for the team's time was 14 and the upper quartile was 18 minutes. Represent this information with a box-and-whisker plot.

Answer

Question 7

The lowest score in the year nine algebra test was 55%. The highest score was 92%. The median was 75%. The lower quartile score was 60% and the upper quartile was 85%. Represent this information with a box-and-whisker plot.

Answer

Question 8

The lowest height in a class was 155cm. The highest height is 191cm. The median height was 173cm. The lower quartile was 164cm and the upper quartile was 182cm.

Represent this information with a box-and-whisker plot.

Answer

Question 9

The lowest score in the mock GCSE English exam was 51%. The highest score was 89%. The median score was 70%. The lower quartile is 60% and the upper quartile is 80%. Represent this information with a box-and-whisker plot.

Answer

Question 10

The quickest time for the school sports day relay teams was 7 minutes. The slowest time was 16 minutes. The median time was 10 minutes. The lower quartile is 8 minutes and the upper quartile is 15 minutes. Represent this information with a box-and-whisker plot.

Answer

Now check your answers before moving onto the next section of the guide.

ANSWERS TO QTS NUMERACY TEST SECTION 21

Q1. The lowest score on a Maths test is 53. The highest score is 92. The median score is 71. The lower quartile is 56 and the upper quartile is 87.

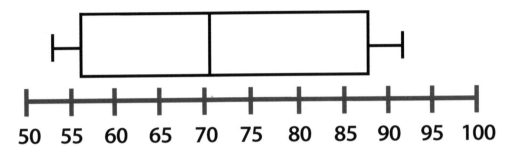

Q2. The lowest score on the year nine History test is 5 out of 20. The highest score was 19. The median score is 11. The lower quartile is 9 and the upper quartile is 15.

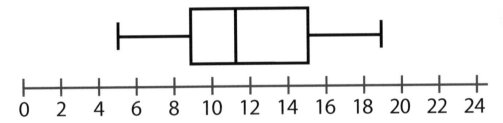

Q3. The lowest score in the year seven Science tests was 65. The highest score was 95. The median score was 80. The lower quartile score was 70 and the upper quartile score was 85.

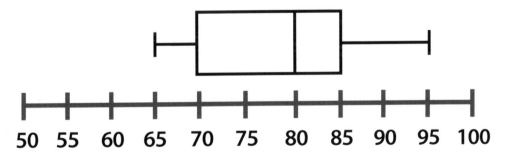

Q4. The lowest percentage for attendance was 51%. The highest attendance was 100%. The median percent for attendance is 70%. The lower
quartile percent was 61% and the upper quartile percent was 90%.

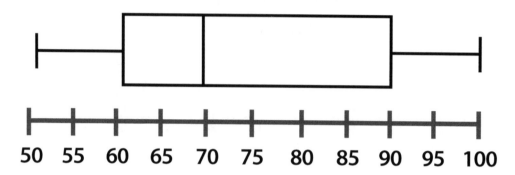

50 55 60 65 70 75 80 85 90 95 100

Q5. The lowest number of golden stars is 0. The highest number is 20. The
median number of golden stars is 11. The lower quartile number is 8 and the
upper quartile number is 16.

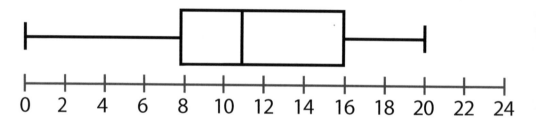

0 2 4 6 8 10 12 14 16 18 20 22 24

Q6. The quickest time for the schools cross country team was 12 minutes.
The slowest time for the team was 22 minutes. The median time was 16
minutes. The lower quartile for the team's time was 14 and the upper quartile time was 18 minutes.

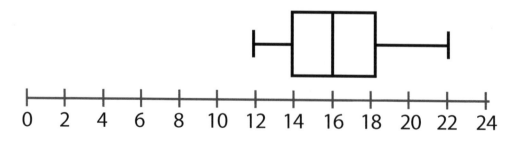

0 2 4 6 8 10 12 14 16 18 20 22 24

Q7. The lowest score in year nine Algebra test was 55%. The highest score was 92%. The median was 75%. The lower quartile score was 60% and the upper quartile was 85%.

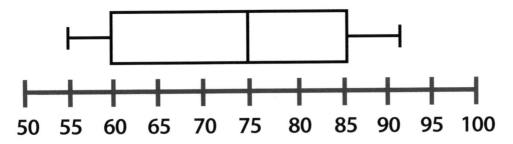

Q8. The lowest height in a class was 155cm. The highest height 191cm. The median height was 173cm. The lower quartile was 164cm and the upper quartile was 182cm.

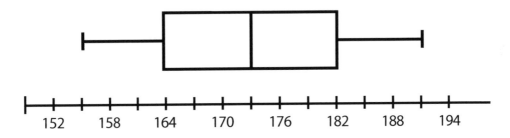

Q9. The lowest score in the mock GCSE English exam was 51%. The highest score was 89%. The median score was 70%. The lower quartile is 60% and the upper quartile is 80%.

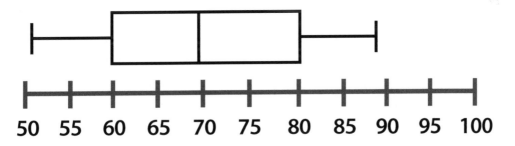

Q10. The quickest time for the school sports day relay teams was 7 minutes. The slowest time was 16 minutes. The median time was 10 minutes. The lower quartile is 8 minutes and the upper quartile is 15 minutes.

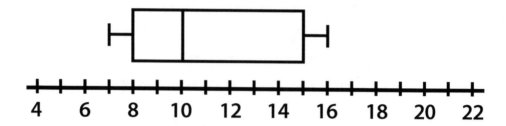

QTS NUMERACY TEST
SECTION 22

*There are 10 questions in this sample test section,
and you have 8 minutes to complete them.*

QTS NUMERACY TEST SECTION 2

Question 1

Test marks in Maths, History and English for Year 9 are compared by three box – and – whisker diagrams shown below. Marks are shown on the vertical axis.

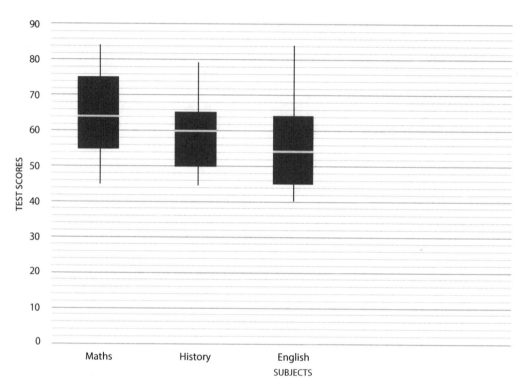

(1) The interquartile range for Maths is higher than that for English. True or false?

[   ]

(2) The lowest mark was in History. True or false?

[   ]

(3) The median score for Maths is 65. True or false?

[   ]

Question 2

Attendance for term 1 in a secondary school are compared by box – and – whisker diagrams shown below. The number of absences are shown on the vertical axis.

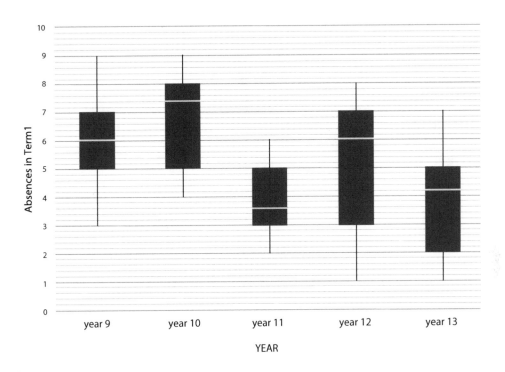

(1)The difference between the median absences between year 9 and 12 is approximately 5. True or false?

(2)The highest number of absences came from year 12. True or false?

(3)The interquartile range for year 10 is higher than that of year 11. True or false?

Question 3

Mock GCSE English results are compared over the years by box and whisker diagrams shown below. The results in percentages are shown on the vertical axis.

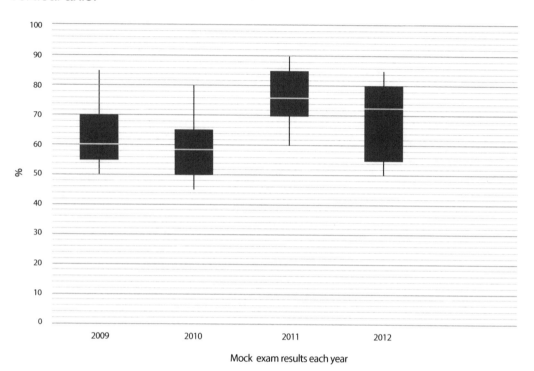

Mock exam results each year

(1)The difference in median results between 2009 and 2011 is approximately by 16%. True or false?

(2)The lowest mark in the mock GCSE English exam was 50%. True or false?

(3)The interquartile range for the years 2009 and 2010 are the same. True or false?

Question 4

Distance travelled by pupils to get to school are compared by the box – and – whisker diagrams shown below. The distance travelled in kilometres is shown on the vertical axis.

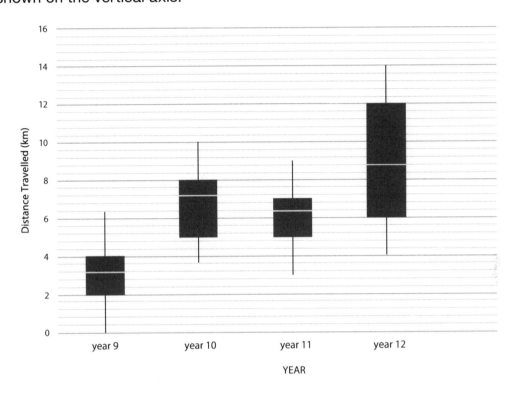

(1)The furthest distance travelled by year 10 is approximately 10km. True or false?

```
┌─────────────┐
│             │
│             │
└─────────────┘
```

(2)The interquartile range for year 9 is higher than that of year 12. True or false?

```
┌─────────────┐
│             │
│             │
└─────────────┘
```

(3)The smallest distance travelled by year 12 is approximately 1km more than the smallest distance travelled by year 10. True or false?

```
┌─────────────┐
│             │
│             │
└─────────────┘
```

Question 5

School reports for Year 9 for English, Maths and Science are compared by box-and-whisker diagrams shown below. The results in percentages are shown on the vertical axis.

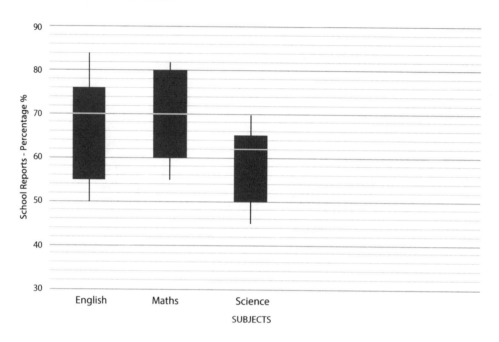

(1)The median percentage for English and Maths are the same. True or false?

(2)In English, the highest percentage is 84%. True or false?

(3)The interquartile range for English is 6% more than the interquartile range for Science

Question 6

A Maths Test is given to three classes. The results are compared by box-and-whisker diagrams shown below. The scores are shown on the vertical axis.

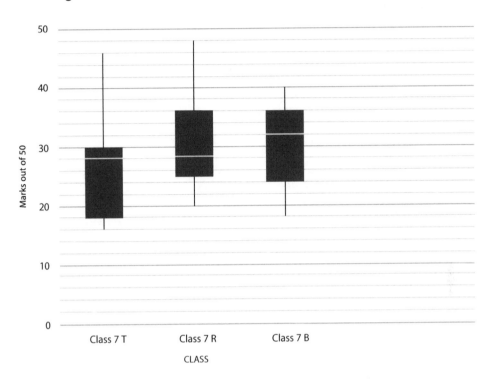

(1)The difference in median scores between class 7 R and B is approximately 4. True or false?

[   ]

(2)The mean mark for the highest scores across all three classes is approximately 45. (Round up to the nearest full number) True or false?

[   ]

(3)The lower quartile range for class 7 R is 20. True or false?

[   ]

Question 7

Cross country results from three different secondary schools were recorded. The results are compared by box-and-whisker diagrams shown below. The time in minutes are shown on the vertical axis.

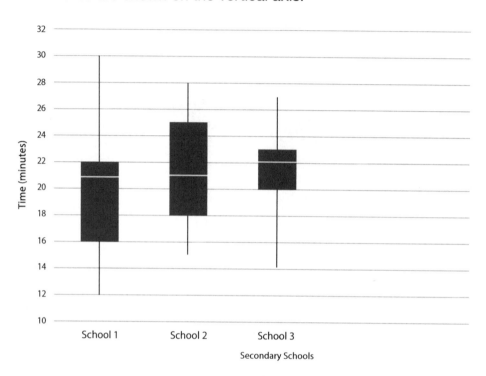

(1) The median time for school 1 and school 2 are the same. True or false?

(2) The interquartile range for school 1 is higher than that of school 2. True or false?

(3) The quickest time for the cross country race was 16 minutes. True or false?

Question 8

Test marks in Maths from three different Maths levels are compared by three box-and-whisker diagrams shown below. Marks are shown on the vertical axis.

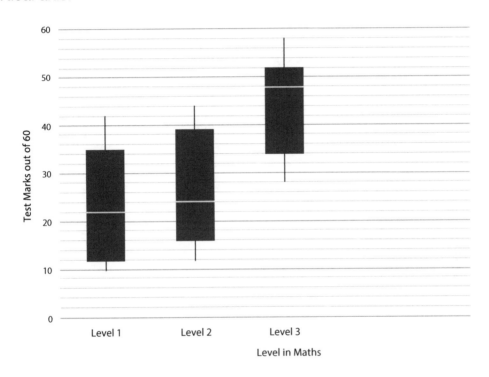

(1)The difference between the median marks for level 1 and level 3 is approximately 26. True or false?

(2)The difference between the highest score overall and the lowest score overall is approximately 50. True or false?

(3)The interquartile range for level 1 is the same as the interquartile range for level 2. True or false?

Question 9

Pupils receive their Geography mock test results and are compared by three box-and-whisker diagrams shown below. Marks out of 100 are shown on the vertical axis.

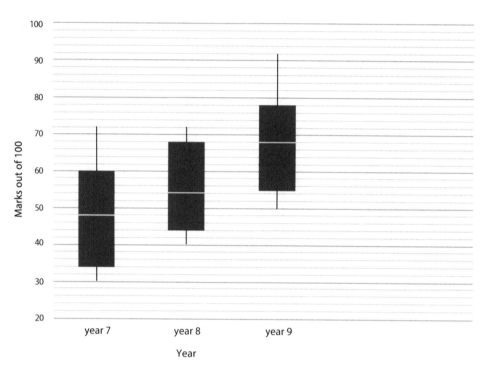

(1) The interquartile range for Year 7 is lower than the interquartile range of Year 8. True or false?

(2) The highest mark for year 8 was 68. True or false?

(3) The difference in the median mark for year 9 is approximately 20 marks more than year 7. True or false?

Question 10

Test grades in History, Geography, Media and English for year 11 are compared by box-and-whisker diagrams shown below. Grades in percentages are shown on the vertical axis.

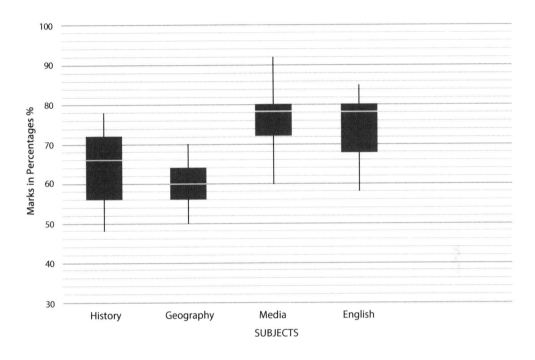

(1)The median range is the same in Media and English. True or false?

(2)Media is year 11's strongest subject. True or false?

3)The interquartile range of Media is higher than that of Geography. True or false?

Now check your answers before moving onto the next section of the guide.

ANSWERS TO QTS NUMERACY TEST SECTION 22

Q1.

(1) True

(2) False

(3) False

Q2.

(1) False

(2) False

(3) True

Q3.

(1) True

(2) False

(3) True

Q4.

(1) True

(2) False

(3) False

Q5.

(1) True

(2) True

(3) True

Q6.

(1) True

(2) True

(3) False

Q7.

(1) True

(2) False

(3) False

Q8.

(1) True

(2) False

(3) True

Q9.

(1) False

(2) False

(3) True

Q10.

(1) True

(2) True

(3) False

QTS NUMERACY TEST
SECTION 23

There are 10 questions in this sample test section, and you have 8 minutes to complete them.

QTS NUMERACY TEST SECTION 23

Question 1

The set of data below shows the results in a year 9 History test for 50 pupils. The marks are out of 10. The teacher wants to find the mean mark for this test. Give your answer to 1 decimal place.

Marks in History Test	No. of pupils	No. of pupils X History Marks
1	5	$1 \times 5 = 5$
2	1	$2 \times 1 = 2$
3	8	
4	2	
5	7	
6	6	
7	3	
8	11	
9	4	
10	3	
Totals	50	

The mean mark is:

Question 2

The set of data below shows the results in a year 8 English pop quiz for 63 pupils. The marks are out of 10. The teacher wants to find the mean mark for this test. Give your answer to 1 decimal place.

Marks in English pop quiz	No. of pupils	No. of pupils X English Marks
1	2	1 X 2 = 2
2	4	2 X 4 = 8
3	6	
4	9	
5	11	
6	6	
7	7	
8	3	
9	9	
10	6	
Totals	63	

The mean mark is:

Question 3

The set of data below shows the work ethic scores of year 7 which is shown on their school report for the academic year. The scores are out of 10. The teacher wants to find the mean work ethic score. Give your answer to 1 decimal place.

Work ethic mark	No. of pupils	No. of pupils X work ethic mark
1	2	1 X 2 = 2
2	4	2 X 4 = 8
3	3	
4	8	
5	9	
6	6	
7	11	
8	5	
9	4	
10	2	
Totals	54	

The mean mark is:

[   ]

Question 4

The set of data below shows the results in a science test for 36 pupils. The marks are out of 20. The teacher wants to find the mean mark for this test. Give your answer to 1 decimal place.

Science test mark	No. of pupils	No. of pupils X science test mark
2	2	2 X 2 = 4
4	1	4 X 1 = 4
6	4	
8	3	
10	4	
12	5	
14	6	
16	4	
18	3	
20	4	
Totals	36	

The mean mark is:

Question 5

The set of data below shows the results in a year 7 P.E test for 45 pupils. The marks are out of 15. The teacher wants to find the mean mark for this test. Give your answer to 1 decimal place.

P.E test marks	No. of pupils	No. of pupils X P.E test mark
1	0	1 X 0 = 0
2	0	2 X 0 = 0
3	4	
4	1	
5	3	
6	1	
7	2	
8	6	
9	3	
10	4	
11	5	
12	6	
13	5	
14	2	
15	3	
Totals	45	

The mean mark is:

Question 6

The set of data below shows the results in a year 10 English exam. The marks are out of 100%. The teacher wants to find the mean mark for this test. Give your answer to 1 decimal place.

English exam (%)	No. of pupils	No. of pupils X English exam (%)
10	0	10 X 0 = 0
20	2	20 X 2 = 40
30	4	
40	5	
50	3	
60	10	
70	8	
80	7	
90	9	
100	6	
Totals	54	

The mean mark is:

Question 7

The set of data below shows the results in a year 11 Media mock exam. The marks are out of 100%. The teacher wants to find the mean mark for this test which was given to 68 pupils. Give your answer to 1 decimal place.

Media mock exam (%)	No. of pupils	No. of pupils X media mock exam (%)
10	0	10 X 0 = 0
20	2	20 X 2 = 40
30	3	
40	6	
50	8	
60	11	
70	8	
80	15	
90	12	
100	3	
Totals	68	

The mean mark is:

Question 8

The set of data below shows the results in a year 12 Cross country race. The pupils were assessed on their time. The teacher wants to find the mean time for the cross country race which 44 pupils took part. Give your answer to 1 decimal place.

Time (minutes)	No. of pupils	No. of pupils X time
8	3	8 X 3 = 24
9	2	9 X 2 = 18
10	4	
11	3	
12	5	
13	2	
14	2	
15	4	
16	6	
17	3	
18	5	
19	3	
20	2	
Totals	44	

The mean time is:

Question 9

The set of data below shows the results of Year 10's sports day long distance run. The pupils were assessed on their time in which 38 pupils took
part. Give your answer to 1 decimal place.

Time (minutes)	No. of pupils	No. of pupils X time (minutes)
8	1	8 X 1 = 8
9	1	9 X 1 = 9
10	3	
11	5	
12	10	
13	8	
14	4	
15	3	
16	2	
17	1	
18	0	
Totals	38	

The mean time is:

226 QTS NUMERACY TESTS

Question 10

The set of data below shows the results of year 10's height order. 42 pupils measured their height. The teacher wants to find the median height in her class. Give your answer to 1 decimal place.

Height (cm)	No. of pupils	No. of pupils X height (cm)
125	3	125 x 3 = 375
130	2	130 x 2 = 260
135	4	
140	3	
145	5	
150	2	
155	2	
160	4	
165	6	
170	3	
175	5	
180	3	
Totals	42	

The mean mark is:

[   ]

Now check your answers before moving onto the next section of the guide.

ANSWERS TO QTS NUMERACY TEST SECTION 23

1. 5.7

2. 5.9

3. 5.6

4. 12.2

5. 9.6

6. 67.4%

7. 67.2%

8. 14 minutes and 2 seconds

9. 12 minutes and 5 seconds

10. 154.4cm

QTS NUMERACY TEST
SECTION 24

There are 10 questions in this sample test section, and you have 8 minutes to complete them.

QTS NUMERACY TEST SECTION 24

Question 1

A Mock exam in Science consists of two papers. The first paper is out of 50 and has weighting of 75% given to it. The second paper is out of 40 and has a weighting of 25% given to it. A pupil gets 44 in the first paper and 27 in the second paper. What is the pupil's final percentage score? Give your answer to 1 decimal place.

Weighted score is:

Question 2

A test in Maths consists of two papers. The first paper is out of 70 and has weighting of 65% given to it. The second paper is out of 60 and has a weighting of 35% given to it. A pupil gets 56 in the first paper and 33 in the second paper. What is the pupil's final percentage score? Give your answer to 1 decimal place.

Weighted score is:

Question 3

A test in Science consists of three papers. The first paper is out of 70 and has weighting of 45% given to it. The second paper is out of 50 and has weighting of 40%. The third test is out of 10 and has weighting of 15%. A pupil gets 56 in the first paper, 20 in the second paper and 8 in the third paper. What is the pupil's final percentage score?

Weighted score is:

Question 4

A test in History consists of three papers. The first paper is out of 80 and has weighting of 35% given to it. The second paper is out of 60 and has weighting of 30%. The third test is out of 40 and has weighting of 35%. A pupil gets 60 in the first paper, 45 in the second paper and 35 in the third paper. What is the pupil's final percentage score? Give your answer to 1 decimal place.

Weighted score is:

┌─────────────────┐
│   │
│   │
└─────────────────┘

Question 5

A pop quiz in Geography consists of two sections. The first section is out of 20 and has weighting of 85%. The second section is out of 15 and has a weighting of 15% given to it. A pupil gets 16 in the first section and 8 in the second section. What is the pupil's final percentage score?

Weighted score is:

┌─────────────────┐
│   │
│   │
└─────────────────┘

Question 6

A quiz in Media consists of three sections. The first section is out of 30 and has weighting of 60%. The second section is out of 20 and has a weighting of 25%. The third section is out of 10 and has weighting of 15%. A team gets 20 in the first section, 12 in the second section and 6 in the third section. What is the pupil's final percentage score?

Weighted score is:

┌─────────────────┐
│   │
│   │
└─────────────────┘

Question 7

A pop quiz is given to teachers regarding general knowledge. It consists of two sections. The first section is out of 50 and has weighting of 55%. The second section is out of 45 and has a weighting of 45% given to it. A teacher gets 48 in the first section and 32 in the second section. What is the teacher's final percentage score?

Weighted score is:

┌─────────────────┐
│   │
│   │
└─────────────────┘

Question 8

A test in Physics consists of three papers. The first paper is out of 50 and has weighting of 45% given to it. The second paper is out of 40 and has weighting of 30%. The third test is out of 20 and has weighting of 25%. A pupil gets 40 in the first paper, 20 in the second paper and 12 in the third paper. What is the pupil's final percentage score?

Weighted score is:

Question 9

A Mock exam in Sociology consists of two papers. The first paper is out of 50 and has weighting of 55% given to it. The second paper is out of 40 and has a weighting of 45% given to it. A pupil gets 46 in the first paper and 22 in the second paper. What is the pupil's final percentage score? Give your answer to 1 decimal place.

Weighted score is:

Question 10

A Mock P.E test consists of theory and practical. The practical is out of 10 and has weighting of 75% given to it. The theory is out of 50 and has a weighting of 25% given to it. A pupil gets 9 in the practical and 36 in their theory. What is the pupil's final percentage score? Give your answer to 1 decimal place.

Weighted score is:

Now check your answers before moving onto the next section of the guide.

ANSWERS TO QTS NUMERACY TEST SECTION 24

1. 82.9%

2. 71.3%

3. 64%

4. 79.4%

5. 76%

6. 64%

7. 84.8%

8. 66%

9. 75.4%

10. 85.5%

QTS NUMERACY TEST
SECTION 25

*There are 10 questions in this sample test section,
and you have 8 minutes to complete them.*

QTS NUMERACY TEST SECTION 25

Question 1

The two way table shown compares pupils' results for GCSE Maths with GCSE Science grades.

Maths GCSE Grades	Science GCSE Grades								
	A*	A	B	C	D	E	F	U	Total
A*									
A			3						3
B	1	2	4	2	3				12
C		2	3	10	2	2		1	20
D			2	3					5
E									
F									
U									
Total	1	4	12	15	5	2		1	40

(1)The Number of pupils who achieved both a C grade in their GCSE Science and their GCSE Maths is 3. True or False?

(2)The number of pupils who got a B grade in Maths is 12. True or false?

(3)The percentage of pupils who received a C grade in Science is approximately 37.5%. True or false?

Question 2

The two way table shown compares pupils' results for GCSE English with GCSE Media grades.

English GCSE Grades	Media GCSE Grades								Total
	A*	A	B	C	D	E	F	U	Total
A*									
A		2	2	3					7
B		1	3	4				1	9
C			8	10	6	1			25
D				1		2			3
E								1	1
F									
U									
Total		3	13	18	6	3		2	45

(1) The number of pupils that received a C grade in English and a C grade in Media is 10. True or false?

```
┌──────────────────┐
│                  │
│                  │
└──────────────────┘
```

(2) The percentage of pupils who received a D grade in Media is approximately 25.4%. True or false?

```
┌──────────────────┐
│                  │
│                  │
└──────────────────┘
```

(3) Over half the pupils received a C grade or above in their Media GCSE. True or false?

```
┌──────────────────┐
│                  │
│                  │
└──────────────────┘
```

Question 3

The two way table shown compares pupils' results for GCSE History with GCSE Geography grades.

| History GCSE Grades | Geography GCSE Grades | | | | | | | | |
	A*	A	B	C	D	E	F	U	Total
A*									
A				2					2
B		2	2	3					7
C			4	17	3	2		2	28
D		3	5		1	1			10
E								1	1
F									
U									
Total		5	11	22	4	3		3	48

(1)Over half the pupils received a C grade or above in History. True or false?

(2)Pupils' who received a C grade in both History and Geography is 4. True or false?

(3)The number of pupils who received an E grade or below in Geography is 1. True or false?

Question 4

The two way table shown compares pupils' results for GCSE P.E with GCSE English grades.

P.E GCSE Grades	English GCSE Grades								Total
	A*	A	B	C	D	E	F	U	
A*									
A	1		1	2					4
B	1	2	3	4					10
C	1	3	6	17	4				31
D		1		3					4
E									
F				1					1
U									
Total	3	6	10	27	4				50

(1)The total number of pupils who received a B grade in P.E is 6. True or false?

(2)The percentage number of pupils who received a C grade in English is approximately 20%. True or false?

(3)Pupils who got a B grade in both P.E and English is 2. True or false?

Question 5

The two way table shown compares pupils' results for Maths Test 1 and Maths Test 2.

Maths Test 1	Maths Test 2								Total
	A*	A	B	C	D	E	F	U	
A*									
A									
B	1	1		1					3
C		2	2	12	1				17
D			5	3	3				11
E			4				1	1	6
F									
U									
Total	1	3	11	16	4		1	1	37

(1)The number of pupils' who achieved a C grade in both the Maths Test 1 and Maths Test 2 is 12. True or false?

(2)The number of pupils who achieved a B grade in the Maths Test 2 is 11. True or false?

(3)The percentage number of pupils who achieved a C grade or above in Maths Test 2 is approximately 84%. True or false? (Round up to the nearest whole number).

Question 6

The two way table shown compares pupils' results for a GCSE Physics test and a GCSE Chemistry test.

GCSE Physics Test	GCSE Chemistry Test								Total
	A*	A	B	C	D	E	F	U	
A*			2						2
A		2	1	1					4
B	1	1	5	10					17
C	1	6	8	1	2				18
D				1					1
E									
F									
U									
Total	2	9	16	13	2				42

(1)The total number of pupils who received a B grade for either Physics or Chemistry is 35. True or false?

(2)The percentage number of pupils who received a C grade in Physics is approximately 42.9%. True or false? (Round up to the nearest whole number).

(3)The number of pupils who received an A* in their Physics test is 2. True or false?

Question 7

The two way table shown compares pupils' results for a GCSE P.E theory test and a GCSE P.E practical test.

GCSE P.E theory	GCSE P.E practical								
	A*	A	B	C	D	E	F	U	Total
A*									
A	1		2	4					7
B	2	2	11	2					17
C	2	3	7	9	2				23
D		1							1
E									
F									
U									
Total	5	6	20	15	2				48

(1)The percentage number of pupil's who received a C grade or above for P.E practical is approximately 75.8%. True or false?

(2)The percentage number of pupil's who received a B grade or above for P.E theory is approximately 50%. True or false?

(3)The number of pupil's who received a B grade for both their practical and theory tests in P.E is 17. True or false?

Question 8

The two way table shown compares pupils' results for an English poetry test and English literature test.

English poetry	English Literature								Total
	A*	A	B	C	D	E	F	U	
A*				3					3
A		2	1	2	2				7
B		3	8	1	1				13
C		1	11	15		2			29
D									
E									
F									
U									
Total		6	20	21	3	2			52

(1)The number of pupils who received a B grade for both English poetry and English Literature is 8. True or false?

(2)Half the pupils received a B grade or above for English Literature. True or false?

(3)3 pupils who received a C grade in English literature also received an A* in English poetry. True or false?

Question 9

The two way table shown compares pupils' results for Science experiment 1 and Science experiment 2.

Science experiment 1	Science experiment 2								
	A*	A	B	C	D	E	F	U	Total
A*									
A				2					2
B		1	3	3	3				10
C		1	2	10	5				18
D		1		2					3
E									
F									
U									
Total		3	5	17	8				33

(1)The number of pupils who achieved a C grade in both experiments is 18. True or false?

[ ]

(2)The number of pupils who got a B grade in Science experiment 2 is 5. True or false?

[ ]

(3)The number of pupils who got a B grade in Science experiment 1 is 10. True or false?

[ ]

Question 10

The two way table shown compares pupils' results for Psychology Test 1 and Psychology Test 2.

Psychology Test 1	Psychology Test 2								
	A*	A	B	C	D	E	F	U	Total
A*									
A	1	1			2				4
B		2	8	1					11
C			6	9	2				17
D			1			2			3
E									
F									
U									
Total	1	3	15	10	4	2			35

(1)The percentage number of pupils who received a D grade or below in the Psychology Test 2 is approximately 22%. True or false?

(2)The number of pupils who received a C grade for the Psychology Test 1 is 17. True or false?

(3)The number of pupils who received a B grade for the Psychology Test 2 is 15. True or false?

Now check your answers before moving onto the next section of the guide.

ANSWERS TO QTS NUMERACY TEST SECTION 25

Q1.

(1) False

(2) True

(3) True

Q2.

(1) True

(2) False

(3) True

Q3.

(1) True

(2) False

(3) False

Q4.

(1) False

(2) False

(3) False

Q5.

(1) True

(2) True

(3) True

Q6.

(1) False

(2) True

(3) True

Q7.

(1) False

(2) True

(3) False

Q8.

(1) True

(2) True

(3) True

Q9.

(1) False

(2) True

(3) True

Q10.

(1) False

(2) True

(3) True

QTS NUMERACY TEST
SECTION 26

*There are 10 questions in this sample test section,
and you have 8 minutes to complete them.*

QTS NUMERACY TEST SECTION 26

Question 1

The pie chart below shows the number of pupils who got a Grade C or above in Science in three different schools.

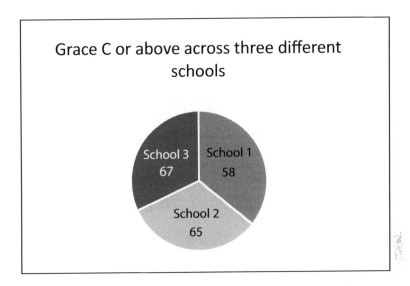

(1)The percentage of pupils who achieved Grade C or above in Science in School 1 compared to all the schools combined was approximately 30.5%. True or false?

(2)The total percentage success at Grade C or above in Science at School 1 and School 2 combined compared to all schools was approximately 64.7%. True or false?

(3)The proportion of pupils getting a grade C or above in Science at School 3 compared to all schools was 67/190. True or false?

Question 2

The pie chart below shows the number of pupils who got a Grade C or above in Maths across four different schools.

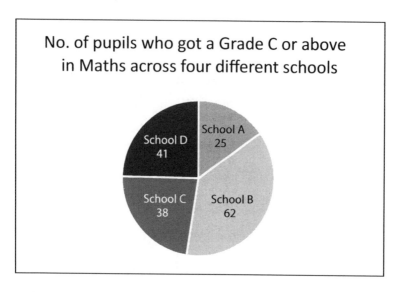

No. of pupils who got a Grade C or above in Maths across four different schools

School A 25

School D 41

School C 38

School B 62

(1)School B has more pupils with a Grade C or above compared to Schools C and A combined. True or false?

(2)Schools D and C have more pupils with a Grade C or above as opposed to Schools A and B combined. True or false?

(3)The total percentage success at Grade C or above in Maths at School B and School C combined compared to all schools was approximately 60%. True or false?

Question 3

The pie chart below shows the number of pupils who averaged 60% or higher in a spelling test across four different schools.

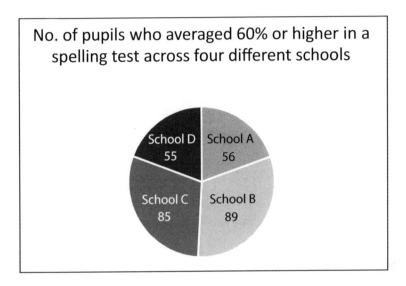

No. of pupils who averaged 60% or higher in a spelling test across four different schools

School D 55
School A 56
School C 85
School B 89

(1)The total percentage success at averaging 60% or higher in a spelling test at School B compared to all schools was approximately 31%. True or false?

(2)Schools D and C have a higher number of pupils combined who averaged 60% or above in the spelling test as opposed to Schools A and B combined. True or false?

(3)In total, there are 285 pupils who averaged 60% or higher in the spelling test. True or false?

Question 4

The pie chart below shows the number of pupils from four teams in Year 8 who have received an award for their school work over the academic year.

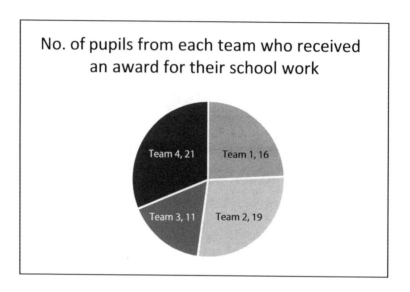

No. of pupils from each team who received an award for their school work

Team 4, 21   Team 1, 16

Team 3, 11   Team 2, 19

(1)There are twice as many pupils who achieved an award for their school work from Team 3 compared to Team 4. True or false?

(2)The total percentage success at receiving an award for their school work in Team 2 compared to all the teams combined was approximately 15.9%. True or false?

(3)Teams 1 and 4 have a higher number of pupils combined than Teams 2 and 3 that received an award for their school work. True or false?

Question 5

The pie chart below shows the number of football tournaments won in the year at four different schools.

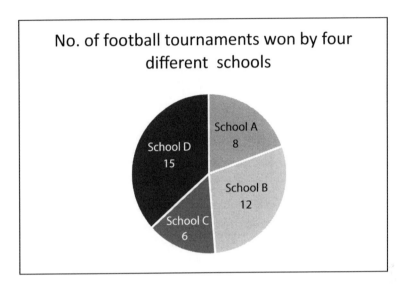

No. of football tournaments won by four different schools

(1)School D won more football tournaments than School A and C combined. True or false?

(2)The percentage of winning games for School C compared to all the winning football tournaments is approximately 14.6%. True or false?

(3)The total percentage of winning football tournaments at School A and School B combined compared to all schools was approximately 48.8%. True or false?

Question 6

The pie chart below shows the number of students whose attendance was 70% or above across four different schools.

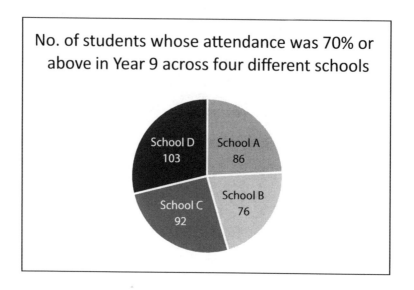

No. of students whose attendance was 70% or above in Year 9 across four different schools

School D 103

School A 86

School B 76

School C 92

(1)The total percentage of students whose attendance was 70% or above in School C and School D combined compared to all schools was approximately 80.4%. True or false?

(2)The percentage of pupils whose attendance was 70% or above in School A compared to all the schools combined was approximately 24.1%. True or false?

(3)The proportion of pupils whose attendance was 70% or above in School D compared to all schools was 103/254. True or false?

Question 7

The pie chart below shows the number of students whose parents are attending parents evening across four different years.

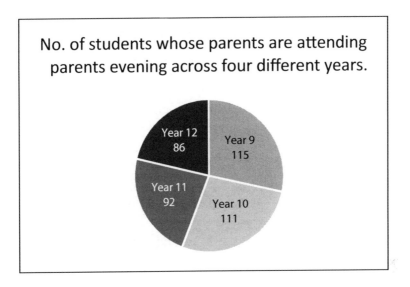

No. of students whose parents are attending parents evening across four different years.

(1)As pupils get older, less parents attend parent's evening. True or false?

(2)The total percentage of students whose parents are attending parents evening in Years 9 and 10 compared to all years was approximately 55.9%. True or false?

(3)In total, there are a total of 400 parents attending parent's evening. True or false?

Question 8

The pie chart below shows the number of students who have booked holidays in term time across four different years.

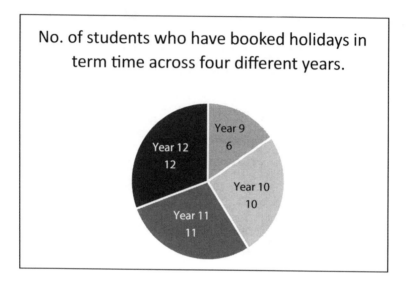

No. of students who have booked holidays in term time across four different years.

(1)As the years progress, students book more time off for holidays. True or false?

(2)The percentage of students who have booked holidays in term time in Year 11 compared to all the years was approximately 28.2%. True or false?

(3)The proportion of pupils who have booked holidays in term time in Year 12 compared to all the years was 4/13. True or false?

Question 9

The pie chart below shows the number of students who have free hot school dinners across four different schools.

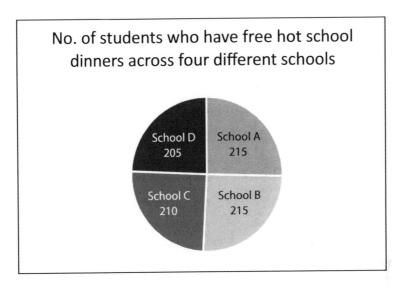

(1)The percentage of students who have free hot school dinners in School A compared to all the schools was approximately 25%. True or false? (Round up to the nearest whole number).

(2)The proportion of pupils who have free hot school dinners in School C compared to all the schools was 40/170. True or false?

(3)The difference between the lowest number of students and the highest number of students who have free hot school dinners is approximately 10. True or false?

Question 10

The pie chart below shows the number of students who received 5 or more GCSES at A- C grade across four different schools.

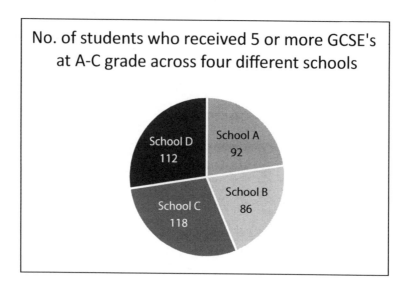

No. of students who received 5 or more GCSE's at A-C grade across four different schools

(1)The proportion of pupils who received 5 or more GCSE's at A-C grade at School B compared to all the schools was 43/204. True or false?

(2)School A and B combined has the same number of students who received 5 or more GCSE's at A-C as Schools C and D combined. True or false?

(3)The percentage of students who received 5 or more GCSE's at A-C grade in School A compared to all the schools was approximately 23%. True or false? (Round up to the nearest whole number).

Now check your answers carefully before moving onto the next section of the guide.

ANSWERS TO QTS NUMERACY TEST SECTION 26

Q1.

(1) True

(2) True

(3) True

Q2.

(1) False

(2) False

(3) True

Q3.

(1) True

(2) False

(3) True

Q4.

(1) False

(2) False

(3) True

Q5.

(1) True

(2) True

(3) True

Q6.

(1) False

(2) True

(3) False

Q7.

(1) True

(2) True

(3) False

Q8.

(1) True

(2) True

(3) True

Q9.

(1) True

(2) False

(3) True

Q10.

(1) True

(2) False

(3) True

QTS NUMERACY TEST
SECTION 27

*There are 10 questions in this sample test section,
and you have 8 minutes to complete them.*

QTS NUMERACY TEST SECTION 27

Question 1

Pupils who succeeded in getting a Maths GCSE at Grade C or above were analysed from 2006 to 2012.

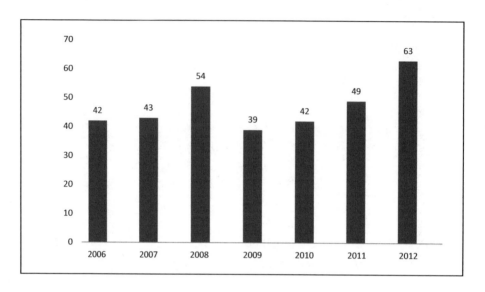

(1)The number of GCSEs at grades C or above increased every year. True or false?

(2)The mean from 2009 to 2012 was 48.25. True or false?

(3)The difference between the lowest percentage of pupils who received a Maths GCSE at C grade or above and the highest is 24. True or false?

Question 2

Pupils who succeeded in getting a Science GCSE at Grade C or above were analysed from 2005 to 2010.

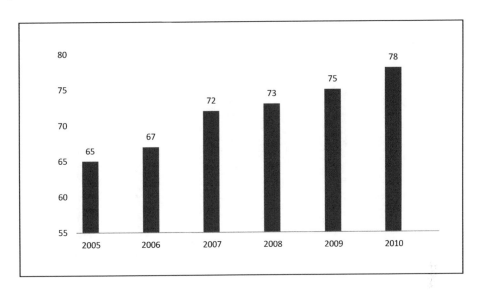

(1) 67 pupils in 2005 succeeded in getting a Science GCSE at Grade C or above. True or false?

(2) The percentage increase from 2005 to 2010 is approximately 20%. True or false?

(3) There was a steady increase of the number of pupils who received a Science GCSE at Grade C or above from 2005 to 2010. True or false?

Question 3

Pupils who succeeded in getting a History GCSE at Grade C or above were analysed from 2004 to 2010.

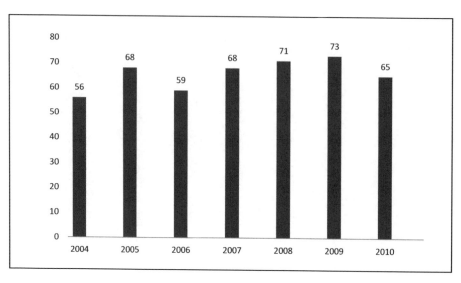

(1)The percentage increase from 2004 to 2009 is approximately 30%. True or false? (Round up to the nearest whole number).

[   ]

(2)The mean from 2005 to 2010 was 67.3. True or false?

[   ]

(3)The difference from the lowest percentage of pupils who received a History GCSE at C grade or above to the highest is 17. True or false?

[   ]

Question 4

Parents who applied for free hot school dinners for their children were analysed from 2003 to 2010.

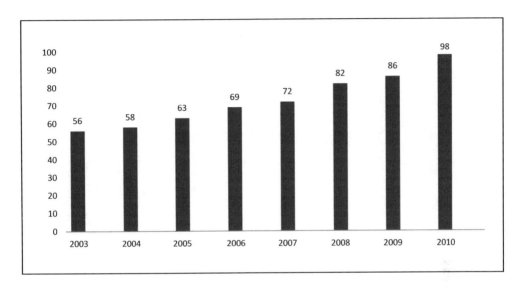

(1)The percentage increase from 2003 to 2010 is approximately 75%. True or false?

(2)The mean from 2005 to 2010 was 78.3. True or false?

(3)There was a steady increase in free hot school dinners between 2003 and 2010. True or false?

Question 5

The number of absences pupils have had in the academic year were analysed between 2005 and 2011.

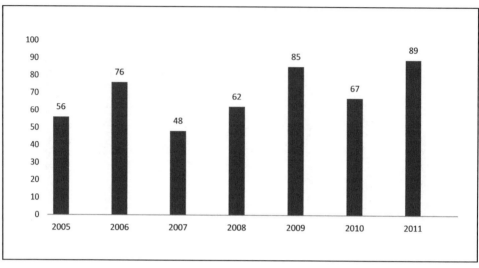

(1)The mean from 2007 to 2011 was 65.2. True or false?

(2)The difference from the lowest to the highest number of absences pupils have had is 40. True or false?

(3)The number of absences pupils have had in the academic year fluctuates each year. True or false?

Question 6

Pupils who attend homework club after school were analysed between 2006 and 2012.

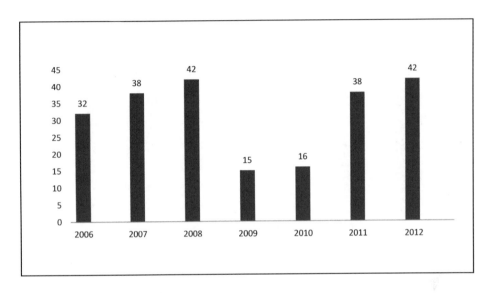

(1)There was a dramatic decrease in the number of pupils who attended homework club after school between the years 2009 and 2010. True or false?

| |
---

(2)The mean from 2008 to 2012 was 30.6. True or false?

| |
---

(3)The difference between the fewest amounts of pupils to the highest amounts of pupils who attend homework club is 32. True or false?

| |

Question 7

Pupils who succeeded in getting a Geography GCSE at Grade C or above were analysed from 2005 to 2010.

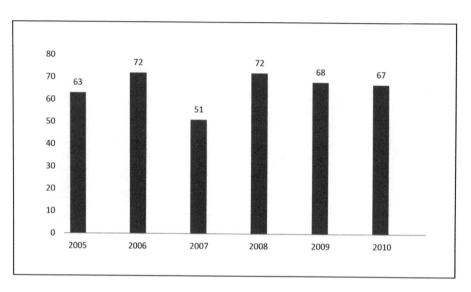

(1)There was a decrease of 21 between 2006 and 2007. True or false?

(2)The mean from 2005 to 2010 was 65.5. True or false?

(3)In total, there were 393 pupils who succeeded in getting a Geography GCSE at C grade or above between 2005 and 2010. True or false?

Question 8

Pupils who are members of an after school team were analysed between 2007 and 2013.

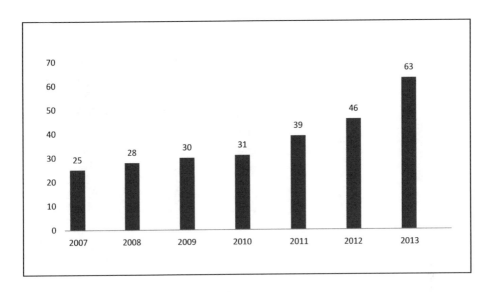

(1)There was a steady increase in the number of pupils who were members of an after school team. True or false?

[ ]

(2)The mean from 2009 to 2013 was 35.6. True or false?

[ ]

(3)The overall average of pupils who are members of an after school team is 37. True or false? (Round up to the nearest whole number).

[ ]

Question 9

Pupils who received gold stars were analysed from 2007 to 2011.

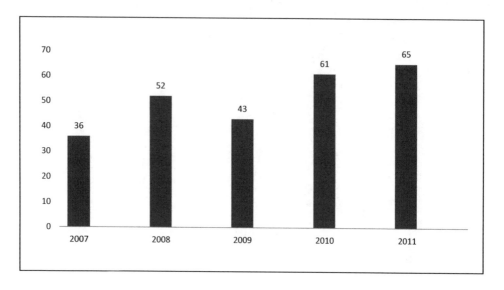

(1)The mean from 2009 to 2011 was 43.6. True or false?

(2)The lowest amount of gold stars occurred in 2009. True or false?

(3)The highest amount of gold stars was awarded in 2011. True or false?

Question 10

Pupils who were put on a school report for lateness were analysed between 2005 and 2010.

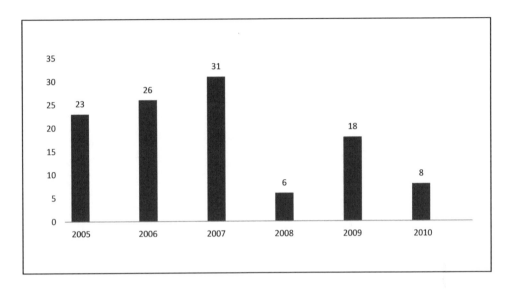

(1)The total number of pupils who were put on a school report for lateness between 2007 and 2009 is 54. True or false?

(2)The difference between 2005 and 2007 regarding how many pupils were put on a school report is 8. True or false?

(3)The mean from 2008 to 2010 is 8. True or false?

Now check your answers before moving onto the next section of the guide.

ANSWERS TO QTS NUMERACY TEST SECTION 27

Q1.

(1) False

(2) True

(3) True

Q2.

(1) False

(2) True

(3) True

Q3.

(1) True

(2) True

(3) True

Q4.

(1) True

(2) True

(3) True

Q5.

(1) False

(2) False

(3) True

Q6.

(1) False

(2) True

(3) False

Q7.

(1) True

(2) True

(3) True

Q8.

(1) True

(2) False

(3) True

Q9.

(1) False

(2) False

(3) True

Q10.

(1) False

(2) True

(3) False

QTS NUMERACY TEST
SECTION 28

There are 10 questions in this sample test section, and you have 8 minutes to complete them.

QTS NUMERACY TEST SECTION 28

Question 1

The head of English created the following table showing the number of pupils in each year group who had additional help in English. What is the percentage of the total number of pupils in all the year groups combined that are having additional tuition. Give your answer rounded to a whole number.

Year Group	No. of pupils	No. of pupils receiving additional help in English
7	96	15
8	108	21
9	111	16
10	98	9
11	116	15

Answer:

Question 2

The head of Science created the following table showing the number of pupils in each year group who had additional help in Science. What is the percentage of the total number of pupils in all the year groups combined that are having additional tuition. Give your answer rounded to a whole number.

Year Group	No. of pupils	No. of pupils receiving additional help in Science
7	104	15
8	112	11
9	96	9
10	103	18
11	101	13

Answer:

Question 3

The head of P.E created the following table showing the number of pupils in each year group who played after school sports. What is the percentage of the total number of pupils in all the year groups combined that played after school sports. Give your answer rounded to a whole number.

Year Group	No. of pupils	No. of pupils who played after school sports
7	92	23
8	103	36
9	111	42
10	99	29
11	116	48
12	112	54

Answer:

Question 4

The head teacher created the following table showing the number of pupils in each year group whose parents are attending parent's evening. What is the percentage of the total number of pupils in all the year groups combined whose parents are attending parent's evening. Give your answer rounded to a whole number.

Year Group	No. of pupils	No. of pupils whose parents are attending parents evening
7	105	96
8	111	85
9	116	76
10	115	83
11	102	56

Answer:

Question 5

The head of English created the following table showing the number of pupils in each year group who got a C grade or above in their test. What is the percentage of the total number of pupils in all the year groups combined that got a C grade or above in their test. Give your answer rounded to a whole number.

Year Group	No. of pupils	No. of pupils who achieved a C grade or above in their English test
7	86	56
8	93	48
9	102	72
10	99	52
11	106	85
12	68	56

Answer:

Question 6

The head teacher created the following table showing the number of pupils in each year group whose attendance was 60% or above. What is the percentage of the total number of pupils in all the year groups combined whose attendance was 60% or above? Give your answer rounded to a whole number.

Year Group	No. of pupils	No. of pupils whose attendance was 60% or above
7	96	82
8	87	71
9	102	98
10	105	90
11	87	72
12	82	79

Answer:

Question 7

The head teacher created the following table showing the number of pupils in each year group whose parents booked a holiday in term time. What is the percentage of the total number of pupils in all the year groups combined whose parents booked a holiday during term time? Give your answer rounded to a whole number.

Year Group	No. of pupils	No. of pupils whose parents booked a holiday during term time
7	116	21
8	121	15
9	103	9
10	95	32
11	87	12

Answer:

Question 8

The head teacher created the following table showing the number of pupils in each year group who received free hot school dinners. What is the percentage of the total number of pupils in all the year groups combined who received free hot school dinners? Give your answer rounded to a whole number.

Year Group	No. of pupils	No. of pupils who received free hot school dinners
7	116	29
8	119	26
9	121	31
10	96	8
11	103	7

Answer:

Question 9

The head teacher created the following table showing the number of pupils in each year group who received detention in one academic year. What is the percentage of the total number of pupils in all the year groups combined that received a detention? Give your answer rounded to a whole number.

Year Group	No. of pupils	No. of pupils who received detention
7	101	46
8	106	31
9	96	20
10	97	17
11	108	5

Answer:

Question 10

The head teacher created the following table showing the number of pupils in each year group who had learning difficulties. What is the percentage of the total number of pupils in all the year groups combined that had learning difficulties? Give your answer rounded to a whole number.

Year Group	No. of pupils	No. of pupils who had learning difficulties
7	94	27
8	97	15
9	103	19
10	87	7
11	93	8

Answer:

Now check your answers before moving onto the next section of the guide.

ANSWERS TO QTS NUMERACY TEST SECTION 28

1. 14%

2. 13%

3. 37%

4. 72%

5. 67%

6. 88%

7. 17%

8. 18%

9. 23%

10. 16%

QTS NUMERACY TEST
SECTION 29

There are 10 questions in this sample test section, and you have 8 minutes to complete them.

QTS NUMERACY TEST SECTION 29

Question 1

Maths GCSE grades were recorded for 40 pupils. The data is shown on a cumulative frequency diagram below. Indicate all true statements below:

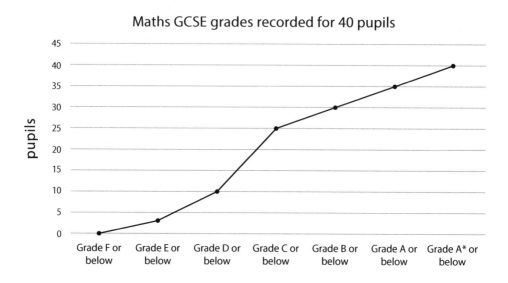

Maths GCSE grades recorded for 40 pupils

(1)15 pupils get above Grade C. True or false?

(2)30 pupils get above Grade D. True or false?

(3)50% of the 40 pupils get a C Grade or above. True or false?

Question 2

English GCSE grades were recorded for 60 pupils. The data is shown on a cumulative frequency diagram below. Indicate all true statements below:

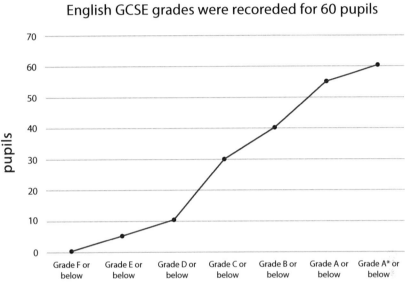

English GCSE grades were recoreded for 60 pupils

(1)The Median grade for the 60 pupils' GCSE grade is grade B or below. True or false?

```
┌─────────────────────┐
│                     │
│                     │
└─────────────────────┘
```

(2)20 pupils achieved a Grade B or above. True or false?

```
┌─────────────────────┐
│                     │
│                     │
└─────────────────────┘
```

(3)5 pupils achieved a Grade D or below. True or false?

```
┌─────────────────────┐
│                     │
│                     │
└─────────────────────┘
```

Question 3

Science GCSE grades were recorded for 50 pupils. The data is shown on a cumulative frequency diagram below. Indicate all true statements below:

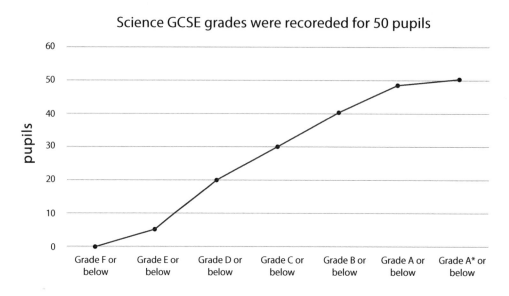

Science GCSE grades were recoreded for 50 pupils

(1)20 pupils received a C Grade or above. True or false?

(2)15 pupils received a D Grade or below. True or false?

(3)No pupils received a Grade F. True or false?

Question 4

P.E scores were recorded for 40 pupils. The data is shown on a cumulative frequency diagram below. Indicate all true statements below:

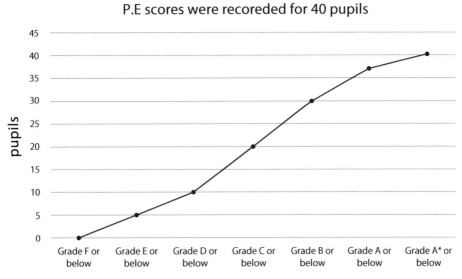

P.E scores were recoreded for 40 pupils

1) The median grade for the 40 pupils is Grade C or above. True or false?

2) 10 pupils received a Grade B or above. True or false?

3) 10 pupils received a Grade E or below. True or false?

Question 5

History grades were recorded for 60 pupils. The data is shown on a cumulative frequency diagram below. Indicate all true statements below:

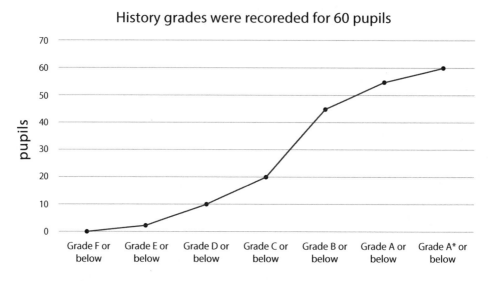

History grades were recoreded for 60 pupils

(1)Over 60% of pupils received a C grade or above. True or false?

(2)15 people received a Grade B or above. True or false?

(3)40 pupils get above a C grade. True or false?

Question 6

The grades were recorded for a Science pop quiz for 30 pupils. The data is shown on a cumulative frequency diagram below. Indicate all true statements below:

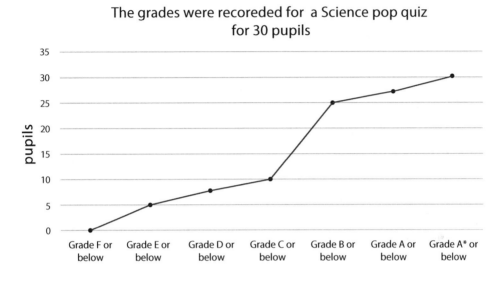

(1)3 pupils achieved a B grade or above. True or false?

(2)15 pupils achieved a C grade or above. True or false?

(3)Over 70% of pupils achieved a C grade or above. True or false?

Question 7

The number of absences 80 pupils have had in a year were analysed between 2006 and 2011. The data is shown on a cumulative frequency diagram below. Indicate all true statements below:

The number of absences pupils have had in a year of 80 pupils from 2006 to 2011

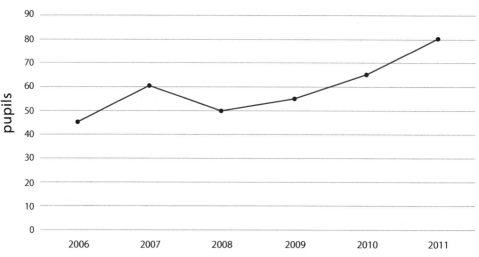

(1)There were no absences in 2011. True or false?

(2)The year 2006 saw the highest amount of absences. True or false?

(3)30 pupils were absent in 2009. True or false?

Question 8

Grades based on English homework were recorded for 50 pupils. The data is shown on a cumulative frequency diagram below. Indicate all true statements below:

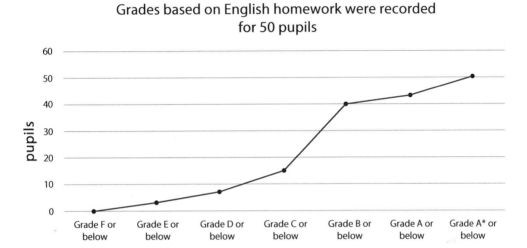

Grades based on English homework were recorded for 50 pupils

(1)1 pupil received a Grade F or below. True or false?

(2)10 pupil received a Grade B or above. True or false?

(3)70% of pupils received a C Grade or above. True or false?

Question 9

The grades were recorded for a Dance performance for 45 pupils. The data is shown on a cumulative frequency diagram below. Indicate all true statements below:

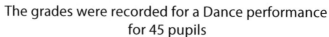

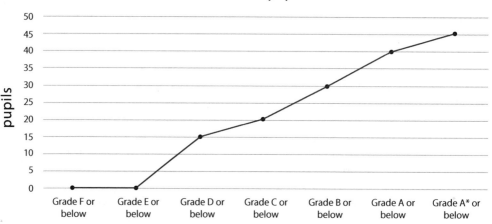

The grades were recorded for a Dance performance for 45 pupils

(1)15 pupils got a Grade D or below. True or false?

(2)Over half the pupils got a Grade C or above. True or false?

(3)30 pupils received a B grade or below. True or false?

Question 10

Geography GCSE grades were recorded for 40 pupils. The data is shown on a cumulative frequency diagram below. Indicate all true statements below:

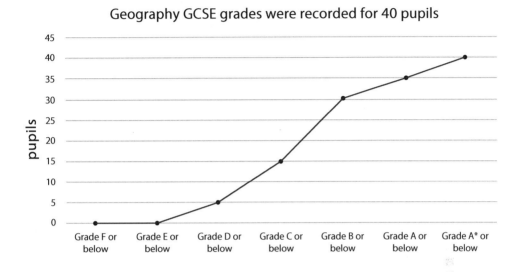

Geography GCSE grades were recorded for 40 pupils

(1)Over 60% of pupils achieved a C Grade or above. True or false?

(2)No pupils received a Grade F. True or false?

(3)30 pupils achieved a D Grade or above. True or false?

Now check your answers before moving onto the next section of the guide.

ANSWERS TO QTS NUMERACY TEST SECTION 29

Q1.

(1) True

(2) True

(3) False

Q2.

(1) False

(2) True

(3) False

Q3.

(1) True

(2) False

(3) True

Q4.

(1) True

(2) True

(3) False

Q5.

(1) True

(2) True

(3) True

Q6.

(1) False

(2) False

(3) False

Q7.

(1) False

(2) False

(3) False

Q8.

(1) False

(2) True

(3) True

Q9.

(1) True

(2) True

(3) True

Q10.

(1) True

(2) True

(3) False

QTS NUMERACY TEST
SECTION 30

*There are 10 questions in this sample test section,
and you have 8 minutes to complete them.*

QTS NUMERACY TEST SECTION 30

Question 1

A teacher represents the relationship between marks in a Maths test and an English test by the scatter graph shown below. The Maths marks are out of 50 and the English marks are out of 20. Indicate all true statements below:

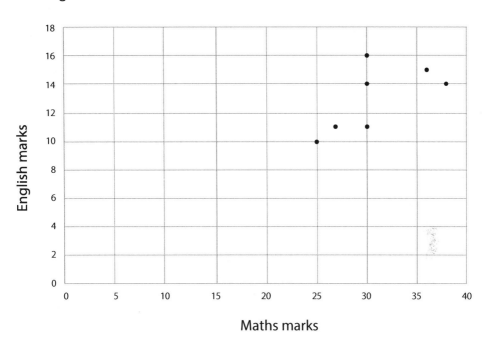

(1)The correlation between Maths and English marks in this test was negative. True or false?

(2)When the pupils mark in Maths was 25, their mark in English was 10. True or false?

(3)The mean mark in the Maths test was approximately 31. True or false?

Question 2

A teacher represents the relationship between marks in a P.E test and an English test by the scatter graph shown below. The P.E marks are out of 20 and the English marks are out of 60. Indicate all true statements below:

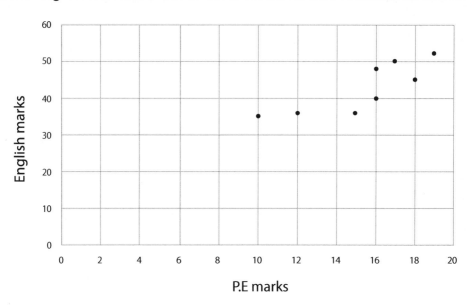

(1)When the pupil's mark in P.E was 18, their English mark was also 18. True or false?

```
[                    ]
```

(2)The correlation between English and P.E marks in this test was positive. True or false?

```
[                    ]
```

(3)In general, if the mark in P.E was high, their mark in English was also high. True or false?

```
[                    ]
```

Question 3

A teacher represents the relationship between marks in a Science Physics test and a Science Chemistry test by the scatter graph shown below. The Physics marks are out of 30 and the Chemistry marks are also out of 30. Indicate all true statements below:

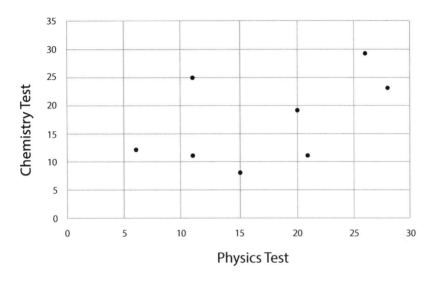

(1)There is no correlation between the marks for the Chemistry and Physics tests. True or false?

(2)When the pupil's mark for Physics was 15, it was also 15 for their Chemistry test. True or false?

(3)The mean mark for the Chemistry test was approximately 17. True or false? (Round up to the nearest whole number).

Question 4

A teacher represents the relationship between marks in a History World War I test and a History World War II test by the scatter graph shown below. The World War I marks are out of 30 and the World War II marks are out of 50. Indicate all true statements below:

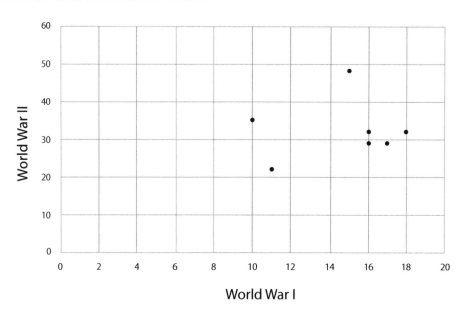

(1)In general, pupils achieved higher marks in the test on World War I. True or false?

[ ]

(2)2 pupils achieved 29 marks for their test on World War II. True or false?

[ ]

(3)When a pupil scored 15 on their test on World War I, they scored 50 on their World War II test. True or false?

[ ]

Question 5

A teacher represents the relationship between marks in a P.E practical test and a P.E theory test by the scatter graph shown below. The P.E practical test is out of 10 and the P.E theory test is out of 40. Indicate all true statements below:

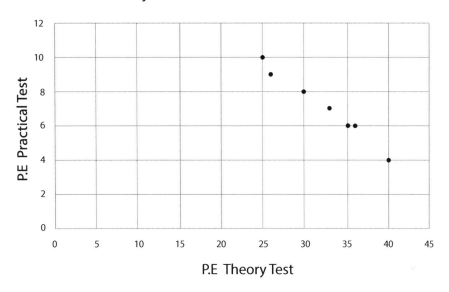

(1)In general, the higher the theory mark, the higher the practical mark. True or false?

(2)The mean mark for the theory test is approximately 32. True or false?

(3)When the pupils mark in their practical test was 10, their theory mark was 25. True or false?

Question 6

A teacher represents the relationship between marks in an English poetry test and an English Shakespeare test by the scatter graph shown below. The poetry test is out of 30 and the Shakespeare test is out of 50. Indicate all true statements below:

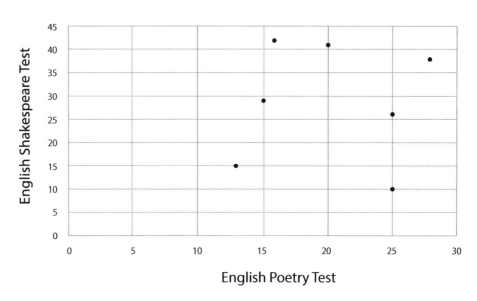

(1)The correlation between the English Shakespeare test and English Poetry test is negative. True or false?

(2)The mean mark for the English Poetry test is approximately 25.75. True or false?

(3)In general, if a pupil's mark was high in English Poetry, it was low in English Shakespeare. True or false?

Question 7

A teacher represents the relationship between marks in Maths Test Paper 1 and Maths Test Paper 2 by the scatter graph shown below. The test paper 1 is marked out of 50, and test paper 2 is also marked out of 50. Indicate all true statements below:

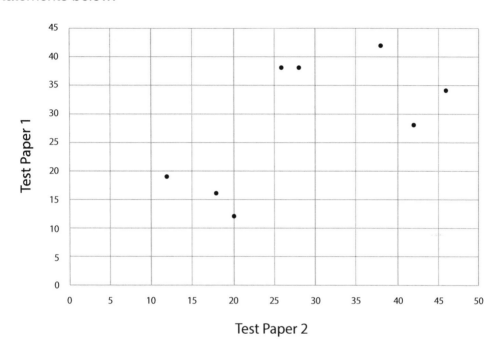

Test Paper 2

(1)The highest mark in Test Paper 1 is 42. True or false?

(2)The lowest mark in Test Paper 2 is 12. True or false?

(3)In general, if the pupil's mark in Test Paper 1 was low, it was also low in Test Paper 2. True or false?

Question 8

A teacher represents the relationship between marks in a Maths test and a Science test by the scatter graph shown below. The Maths test is out of 100 and the Science test is also out of 100. Indicate all true statements below:

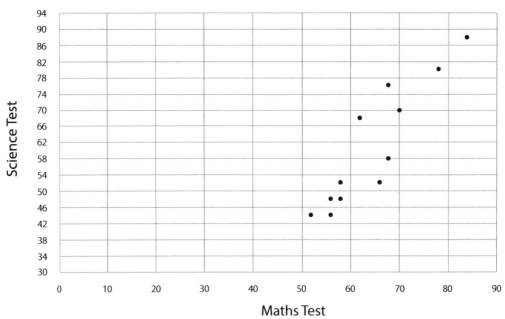

(1)In general if a pupil's mark was high in Science it was also high in Maths. True or false?

(2)The correlation between Maths and Science marks in this test was negative. True or false?

(3)When the pupil's mark in Maths was 70, the corresponding mark in Science was also 70. True or false?

Question 9

A teacher represents the relationship between marks in a Media Studies test and a Film Studies test by the scatter graph shown below. The Media studies test is out of 60 and the Film studies test is out of 50. Indicate all true statements below:

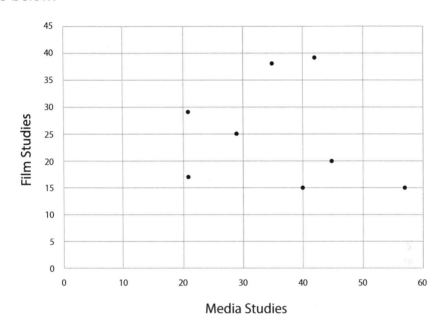

(1)There is no correlation between the Media and Film studies grades. True or false?

[   ]

(2)When the pupil's mark in Film Studies was 25, their mark in Media Studies was 30. True or false?

[   ]

(3)The mean mark for Media Studies was approximately 36. True or false? (Round up to the nearest whole number).

[   ]

Question 10

A teacher represents the relationship between marks in a pop quiz for English Literature and a pop quiz in English Language by the scatter graph shown below. The English Literature test is out of 20 and the English Language test is out of 30. Indicate all true statements below:

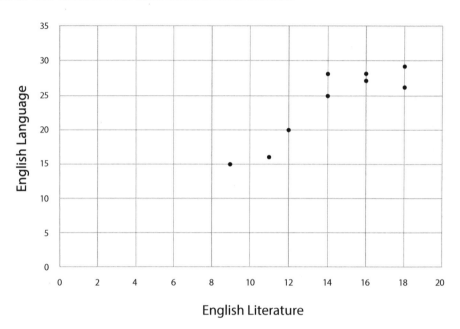

English Literature

(1)In general, the higher the mark in English Literature, the higher the mark in English Language. True or false?

[   ]

(2)The lowest mark in English Language was 9. True or false?

[   ]

(3)The highest mark in English Literature was 18. True or false?

[   ]

Now check your answers carefully.

ANSWERS TO QTS NUMERACY TEST SECTION 30

Q1.

(1) False

(2) True

(3) True

Q2.

(1) False

(2) True

(3) True

Q3.

(1) True

(2) False

(3) True

Q4.

(1) False

(2) True

(3) False

Q5.

(1) False

(2) True

(3) True

Q6.

(1) False

(2) False

(3) False

Q7.

(1) True

(2) True

(3) True

Q8.

(1) True

(2) False

(3) True

Q9.

(1) True

(2) False

(3) True

Q10.

(1) True

(2) False

(3) True

A FEW FINAL WORDS

You have now reached the end of the testing guide and no doubt you will be ready to take your QTS numeracy skills tests.

The majority of candidates who pass the selection process for their chosen career have a number of common attributes. These are as follows:

1. They believe in themselves.

The first factor is self-belief. Regardless of what anyone tells you, you can pass your tests and get the job that you really want. Just like any test, interview or selection process, you have to be prepared to work hard in order to be successful. Make sure you have the self-belief to pass the test with high scores and fill your mind with positive thoughts.

2. They prepare fully.

The second factor is preparation. Those people who achieve in life prepare fully for every eventuality and that is what you must do when you prepare for your QTS skills test. Work very hard and especially concentrate on your weak areas.

3. They persevere.

Perseverance is a fantastic word. Everybody comes across obstacles or setbacks in their life, but it is what you do about those setbacks that is important. If you fail at something, then ask yourself 'why' you have failed. This will allow you to improve for next time and if you keep improving and trying, success will eventually follow. Apply this same method of thinking when you prepare for your test.

4. They are self-motivated.

How much do you want this job? Do you want it, or do you really want it?

When you apply for any job you should want it more than anything in the world. Your levels of self-motivation will shine through on your application, whilst sitting the test and also during your interview. For the weeks and months leading up to the selection process, be motivated as best you can and always keep your fitness levels up as this will serve to increase your levels of motivation.

Work hard, stay focused and be what you want...

Richard McMunn

P.S. Don't forget, you can get FREE access to more tests online at:

www.PsychometricTestsOnline.co.uk

how2become

Get more books, manuals, online tests and training courses at:

www.How2Become.com